THE ABSOLUTENESS OF CHRISTIANITY
AND THE HISTORY OF RELIGIONS

RESEARCH IN THEOLOGY

THE ABSOLUTENESS OF CHRISTIANITY AND THE HISTORY OF RELIGIONS

BY

ERNST TROELTSCH

INTRODUCTION BY
JAMES LUTHER ADAMS

TRANSLATED BY
DAVID REID

JOHN KNOX PRESS
Richmond, Virginia

A translation of Ernst Troeltsch's *Die Absolutheit des Christentums und die Religionsgeschichte: Vortrag gehalten auf der Versammlung der Freunde der Christlichen Welt zu Mühlacker am 3. Oktober 1901. Erweitert und mit einem Vorwort versehen* [The Absoluteness of Christianity and the History of Religions: A Lecture Delivered at a Meeting of Friends of the *Christian World* at Mühlacker on October 3, 1901. Expanded and Accompanied by a Foreword], 3. Aufl. (Tübingen: Verlag von J. C. B. Mohr [Paul Siebeck], 1929).

© John Knox Press 1971
Library of Congress Catalog Card Number: 74-133242
International Standard Book Number: 0-8042-0462-4
Printed in the United States of America

CONTENTS

INTRODUCTION

Sometime during the course of World War II the United States War Department brought together a selected group of cultural anthropologists in order to secure their counsel regarding the management of psychological warfare in face of German National Socialism. After the group had assembled in Washington one of their number asked what the War Department really expected of these men. He explained that in his work the cultural anthropologist for the sake of scientific objectivity presupposes the point of view of cultural relativism, and that therefore he entertains no biases or ethical preferences, in short, that he is not accustomed to making value judgments regarding the various cultures he studies. He went on to say that if the Germans preferred Nazism, they were entitled to that preference, just as democratic Americans are entitled to their own different preference. In either case, he said, the preference is simply an expression of a cultural milieu.

The cultural anthropologist Robert Redfield, commenting subsequently on the colloquy, pointed out that although the attitude of ethical neutrality is an appropriate element in scientific method, it certainly may not be adopted as a way of life appropriate for responsible human beings. Moreover, he said, a decision in favor of ethical neutrality (or its opposite) is a personal decision not to be confused with or derived from cultural relativism considered as an element of objective scientific method.

Ernst Troeltsch (1865–1923) was occupied with questions such as these from the beginning to the end of his career, to be sure changing his views somewhat in the course of his studies. It would be difficult to name any theologian of the first quarter of the present century who has more successfully brought these issues to the fore. It is true that due to a major shift in theological perspectives in Germany he was in wide circles under a cloud for a generation. In recent years, however, his writings have enjoyed a marked revival of interest.

The work that lies before us in the excellent translation of Dr. David Reid belongs to an early period of his publications. The author characteristically displays here a remarkable ability to explore the many facets of an idea or a historical phenomenon, and also to enter into vigorous discussion regarding a wide variety of opposing views.

Troeltsch would have seen in the colloquy in Washington a sign of a major modern revolution that has affected all spheres of life—the arts, law, and religion as well as the sciences. In his view this revolution has come about as a consequence of the appearance of a new historical consciousness that recognizes the contingent and singular character of the events of history. Out of this new historical consciousness has developed the modern historical method.

So profound have been the influences of this method that Troeltsch asserts that the new historical consciousness has determined the character of our epoch which represents "a unique type of culture." Of special significance is the fact that the findings and presuppositions of the historical method have given a body-blow to traditional Christianity. This blow of course has also struck other traditional positions. For the churches it radically called into question Christianity's claim to absolute authority and its claim to have reached "absolute form, i.e., the complete and exhaustive realization of its principle." Troeltsch was convinced that if Christianity could not face the challenge squarely, it would have to retreat into the stagnant cave of obscurantism.

What, then, are the major assumptions and ingredients of the historical method as Troeltsch formulates them? It will assist the reader if we note here that in an essay on "Historical and Dogmatic Method in Theology" published in 1900, two years before the appearance of the present work, Troeltsch set forth his conception of the assumptions and consequences of modern historical method. These assumptions, we should add, figure not only in the present work but also in most of his other writings, including his monumental, unfinished study of *Der Historismus und seine Probleme* (1922) and his last book, which has appeared in English under the title *Christian Thought: Its History and Application* (1923).

In the essay of 1900 he emphasizes three aspects of historical method: the habit of mind associated with historical criticism; the importance of analogy in the study of history; and the correlation or interaction obtaining among all historical events.

(1) The historical habit of mind is a highly critical one that places all traditions under scrutiny, though it aims also to approach the data with empathetic understanding. Here the independence and autonomy of the historian are indispensable. This ideal stems from the Enlightenment as interpreted, for example, by Kant. Moreover, the historical habit of mind presupposes that in the realm of history only judgments of probability are possible, a view that had been stressed by Lessing in the eighteenth century.

(2) The sense of probability regarding historical events depends upon the capacity of the historical critic to discern analogy between what happens before his eyes or within him and the events of the past. Analogy enables the historian to interpret "the unknown of the past by the known of the present." Thus it provides the opportunity to discern a qualified similarity in face of the buzzing, blooming confusion and the dissimilarities of history.

(3) The principle of analogy is related to a third aspect of historical method, the principle of correlation, the assumption that "all historical happening is knit together in a permanent correlation . . . Any one event is related to all others." Therefore, "the historical and the relative are identical." This principle and the principle of analogy bring all of history into a common arena, or, as Troeltsch says, they provide a method of "leveling" all historical phenomena.

A basic feature of history is the singularity, the individuality, the nonrecurrence of events. Troeltsch denies, for example, that there is a permanent "core" in historical Christianity. This is an aspect of history initially stressed by Romanticism. It was Schleiermacher who coined the catchword "individual." Individuality and relativity attach not only to the object of historical studies but also to the subject, the historian. All of these principles of course must take into account the unceasing development—the dynamics, the novelty, the freedom, the unpredictability—of the historical process. In this respect Troeltsch is the Heraclitus of historiography.

His genius is most evident in his recognition of and respect for the multiformity and individuality of cultural phenomena, and in his search for structure and dynamics within these phenomena in terms of which he can identify and interpret standards of truth and value. Coupled with these two concerns is his unrelenting effort to discern some transcendent meaning precisely within the multiformity of culture, and thus to overcome what he calls "unlimited" or "purposeless" relativism.

For Troeltsch the historical method does not imply cultural relativism, except in the sense that "all historical phenomena are unique, individual configurations acted on by influences from a universal context that comes to bear on them in varying degrees of immediacy." This kind of cultural relativism, as the comments reported from Robert Redfield also suggest, is quite different from ethical relativism in the sense that the claim is made that no reasonable basis exists for preferring one thought or action to another. The latter view, which Troeltsch calls "aimless relativism," does not automatically follow from relativism in the first sense.

This second kind of relativism is a matter of choice, and it may be opposed in the name of philosophical or religious reflection and decision. Some such decision is made, at least implicitly, whether one asserts that all cultures should be held in respect as possessing truth or value, or that all cultures are equally valid in the functional sense, or that "every epoch is immediate to God" (Ranke), or that the question of validity is meaningless, *une affaire de géographie* (to use the phrase of Rousseau).

*   *   *

In the present work Troeltsch, as the title suggests, centers attention on the crisis brought upon absolute religious claims by the study of the history of religions. In this study one finds that the different religions make similar or identical claims (though from differing perspectives). Claim stands against claim, and therefore these claims cancel each other. In face of this situation Troeltsch in the earlier essay asserts that "the historical method has acted as a leaven transforming everything and ultimately exploding the structures of all the earlier theological methods."

He gives attention to two of these earlier methods which must now be rejected. The first of these methods, in order to find sanction for absolute authority, appeals to miracle, either as an external event or as an internal one in the form of conversion. But, strictly speaking, these are not historical events. In appealing to them the apologist separates these miracles from the remainder of history, thus creating an island outside the stream of history.

More significant for those who are in sympathy with the modern historical consciousness is the second way that must be rejected, a way that finds its analogue in certain doctrines of progress and also in the writings of Schleiermacher and Hegel. This is the way of speculative philosophy which in its Hegelian form claims that Christianity is "the absolute religion." (The use of the word "absolute" in this context appears to have begun with Hegel.) This form of apologetics ostensibly adopts the historical viewpoint. So far from isolating Christianity from the historical stream or from the other religions, it seeks to demonstrate that in Christianity one can discern the realization of the universal "idea" of religion, the "idea" that finds expression in different and preliminary articulations in the other major religions. All of these religions are said to be in a dialectical evolutionary development culminating in Christianity, and the "idea" is taken to be a norm for the assessment of these other religions in a graded series resembling "a religious geology." Troeltsch's exposition and critique of Hegel's view is an extraordinarily cogent one, comparable to his later appreciation and critique of Marx (in the 1922 volume on historicism). He clearly admires Hegel's effort to provide a philosophical and systematic reflection on the dynamics of history, yet all the more severely does he criticize him for his failure to meet the demands of historical method. Hegel manipulates and distorts the historical data so as to make them fit into his Procrustean framework. Imposition from the outside is evident especially in Hegel's presentation of the history of religions as a linear development, whereas in actuality the evolution of the various religions has taken place in parallel development. Thus Hegel is able to present a spurious conception of "the absolute religion" manifest in the evolutionary process culminating in Christianity (and that means, in Hegel's philosophy of history). Actually, however, if the evolutionary process is to be taken as the foundation, then one should wait until the end of history to discover "the absolute religion." For Troeltsch, then, Hegel's "rainbow of speculation" turns out to be a philosophical substitute for the apologetics of supernaturalistic theology. All of these methods interpret history in terms of a factor coming from outside history. So much for these "absolute-claim theologies."

How, then, should one properly employ historical method? Troeltsch's answer is that one must look at the religions of the world in all of their relativity and singularity, recognizing that all of them are purely historical phenomena with all the conditionings of individual and interrelated phenomena. The task of the theologian is to enter "hypothetically" into these phenomena, comparing the religions and their norms with each other. The goal of the task is to discover a norm in terms of which one may evaluate and rank the major religions, and also to determine the sense, if any, in which the concept of the absolute may be appropriate. In undertaking this task Troeltsch presupposes that one must pass beyond the realm of scientific historical method to the realm of personal decision and faith. In this fashion he aims to "overcome history with history" (to use a phrase from his later writings), that is, to overcome unlimited relativism by historical decision based on norms drawn from empirical history. In carrying out the enterprise of identifying a norm for this end he intends to re-define the concept of the absolute in a fashion compatible with historical method.

It is not possible here, except in long strides, to retrace the steps by which Troeltsch comes to identify a norm for the assessment of the high religions. Through comparing them he finds the distinctive, and probably unsurpassable, element of Christianity to be a history-transforming "personalism." In the teachings of the prophets and Jesus, both God and man in face of nature are elevated into the sphere of personality where unconditional value is realized. Only Christianity has disclosed "a living deity who is act and will"; in Christianity the soul is "set to work in the world for the upbuilding of a kingdom of pure personal values, for the upbuilding of the Kingdom of God."

Viewing the history of religions in terms of this norm, Troeltsch says that Christianity is not only "the high point" but also "the convergence-point of all the developmental tendencies that can be discerned in religion." (It is not clear how Christianity is this sort of "convergence point"; here he seems to adopt a relativized Hegelianism.) In his last book, *Christian Thought* (p. 21), he summarizes the conclusion of the present work by saying of Christianity that "it is the loftiest and most spiritual revelation we know at all. It has the highest validity."

This is a somewhat surprising statement to come from one who set out to look objectively at the history of religions in search of a general norm. He decides that his own piety is the norm in terms of which to assess all religions, including Christianity. This norm is in the main an abstraction from, or perhaps we should say a revision of, his earlier Ritschlian heritage.

The selection of this norm, Troeltsch asserts, is in no way precluded by historical method, for the norm is drawn from among the singularities of history, and it does not flaunt the principle of analogy. Moreover, Christianity as an actual religion in history remains a relative and changing phenomenon. And he makes no absolute claim for it or for the norm. The norm is simply his (constructive) choice. It is valid *for him,* and it can be for others who cherish this heritage. As we shall see, however, it does not invalidate the choices made from the traditions of other religions, so long as they do not make absolute claims.

What, then, of the absolute religion? Troeltsch asserts that Christianity as he interprets it is not an absolute but rather a normative religion. It is inconceivable, however, that the personalistic norm can ever be surpassed.

Troeltsch comes now to a highly significant consequence of his studies. The problem, he says, is not that of making an either-or choice between relativism and absolutism but that of combining the relative and the absolute. This kind of synthesis is what the authentic historical and religious mentality should seek. The absolute must be discerned always in inextricable connection and in relentless tension with the relative, and not in some abstraction. But history is no place for absolute religions or personalities. "To wish to possess the absolute in an absolute way at a particular point in history is a delusion." Absolute truth can appear in unambiguous purity only beyond history or at the end of it. Yet, the relative points beyond itself to the unconditional. Dr. Reid, it seems to me, rightly translates the word *Das Notwendige* as *the unconditional* (words that can be traced at least as far back as Plato). Troeltsch concludes this section of the book with this notable formulation, "In the relative we will find a token of the absolute that transcends history."

The formulations just cited have become common coinage in wide circles today. They anticipate, for example, those of Barth, those of Tillich who speaks of the unconditional and of the paradoxical immanence of the transcendent, reminiscent of those of Luther and Nicholas of Cusa, and those of Reinhold Niebuhr who speaks of the meaning of history which lies beyond history. Sometimes Troeltsch speaks also of new relations between the absolute and the relative as issuing from the depths, "the creative core," of reality. Here we encounter what he calls "the turn to the metaphysical." In this connection he says that the problem is that of discerning, in the relative, tendencies toward the absolute goal, or more accurately, that of working out "a lasting, fresh, and creative synthesis that will give the absolute the form possible to it at a particular moment, and yet remain true to its inherent limitation as a mere approximation of true, ultimate, and universally valid values." This formulation is very close to what Tillich will later call *the Kairos.* In the light of what has been said about historical method and of what Troeltsch says here about the relation between the relative and the unconditional we can readily see the reasons why Tillich was wont to say that Troeltsch is the presupposition and starting point for the contemporary theologian's reflection on the philosophy of history and on the problem of ethical relativism. H. Richard Niebuhr's writings show that he explicitly agreed with Tillich here. (He wrote his doctoral dissertation on Troeltsch's philosophy of religion in 1924.)

* * *

The criticisms of Troeltsch's book have been legion. From the perspective of the historian of religions no proper objection can be raised on the ground that he writes about Christianity from the vantage point of an insider or on the ground that he writes from a particular point of view in this respect. But one can properly object that in treating the other religions he does not allow the representatives to speak from the outside with respect to Christianity.

From the side of the theologians the criticisms of the book have been varied and severe, particularly by those who see in it the last gasp of an enervated liberalism that has lost touch with authentically Christian ("main-line") theology, orthodox or neo-orthodox. Accordingly, it is said that his norm is based on a "liberal reduction" of Jesus which ignores Christology. Thus he speaks of the self-consciousness of Jesus in such a way as to ignore the doctrine of his person. As a consequence, it is argued, his norm is a Christless Christianity. Whether or not Troeltsch represents a moribund liberalism, we must remind these theological critics that his view of Jesus is quite in accord with the current trend in New Testament scholarship which views the Christomonism of neo-Reformation theology as not only a threat to historical scholarship but also as having attempted to impose early

Christian theology on Jesus. Troeltsch asserts that "whatever role messianism may have played in the preaching of Jesus, by and large the person of Christ retired behind the reality" which he proclaimed, "the Kingdom of God." It is not too much to say that current New Testament scholarship largely agrees in saying that Jesus did not identify himself in a clearly messianic or christological fashion, and that his concern was for the new age and the judgment, that is, for the imminence of the Kingdom of God.

Another criticism that can be directed at his formulation of the norm is that he makes little explicit reference to social-institutional aspects of "personalism." Perhaps this failure is to be explained by the fact that only later did he enter into his association with the sociologist Max Weber or into his encounter with Marxist thought. From Weber, he says, he "learned a new way of seeing things." These social-institutional aspects are readily evident in his later work on *The Social Teaching of the Christian Churches.* Troeltsch's greater awareness of them made him take less of a merely literary attitude to the study of the history of religions. He came to see that all high religions in the course of their development "have entered into a union with historical cultures which no effort to displace the religious faith with the intent to substitute for it another one can effectively or justifiably dissolve." [1]

Troeltsch's conception of the role of analogy in historical method has been called radically into question during the past half-century, especially by Karl Barth in *The Epistle to the Romans* (1918) and more recently by Richard R. Niebuhr and Wolfhart Pannenberg—all of these for differently formulated reasons but generally in favor of the authenticity of the resurrection. One should add here that writings on historical method during the past generation have revealed that the method must be more complicated than Troeltsch conceived it to be.

*   *   *

It remains now to ask the question whether Troeltsch overcame religious and ethical relativism. The question cannot be satisfactorily dealt with if one confines attention to the present work. In a lecture on "The Place of Christianity among the World Religions" (1923), already referred to, written for delivery in England but never delivered by reason of his untimely death, he not only summarizes the present work but also states a change of position. In this revised statement he says that he has been "more forcibly" impressed every day by the significance for history of the concept of individuality. Thus he takes more seriously than before the social conditioning of religion. He therefore comes to hold that what is "nobly common to mankind and universally valid . . . is at bottom exceedingly little." Here he seems to push the "uniquity" of historical phenomena to the extreme. Nevertheless, he retains the conviction that standards of truth and value in the various high religions are valid for them, and that the Christian standards are "valid for us." "Each of the faiths," he says, "may experience its contact with the divine life."

This position has been called nominalistic, unlimited relativism. It has also been called a form of henotheism. It is neither of these. Rather, it is analogous to the view set forth by Nicholas of Cusa in *The Vision of God* (1453). Here in Neoplatonic fashion God is symbolized by an omnivoyant human portrait that faces directly the various people who simultaneously confront it, each of them experiencing the directness of his gaze. Cusa calls the portrait "the icon of God." Troeltsch from a somewhat similar perspective asks the question, "Who will presume to make a really final pronouncement?" And he replies, "Only God himself, who has determined their differences, can do that." Thus he combines an acute relativism with a sense of the transcendent meaning of the relative when he says that "a truth which, in the first instance, is *a truth for us* does not cease thereby to be very truth and life."

This is not the solution to the problem of relativism the faithful look for who are in search of universality and certainty. But to them Troeltsch asserts that the absolute cannot be domesticated. History is no place for absolutes. Yet, the faithful of the various religions may in faith enjoy the certainty that God is in his heaven; at the same time they must in humility rejoice that "in my Father's house there are many mansions." But we cannot leave the matter there.

*   *   *

Troeltsch undertook to deal with the problem of relativism in order to come to terms with the modern historical consciousness. Since Troeltsch's time, however, the world situation has changed rapidly. The representatives of the various religions are by technology being forced more and more to enter into personal intercourse and association. We today have entered into an epoch different from that of Troeltsch, one in which universal history is becoming a reality. The new closeness of contact between the religions is one that we experience in our classrooms, in business, political, and cultural exchanges, and also in observing the converts among the youth to one or another of the Oriental faiths. At the same time the traditional conception of missions, as Troeltsch anticipated, is being abandoned. The missionary does not set out merely to convert. He is attempting to listen as well as to tell forth. The spread of Marxism has gradually imported into the Eastern countries a historical consciousness previously more characteristic of the West.

As the worldwide community is becoming more and more a part of our daily lives and contacts, we are destined, as Wilfred Cantwell Smith has argued in an unpublished paper, to participate increasingly in each other's social systems and thus eventually even in each other's ethical and religious perspectives. In this connection Troeltsch would agree with Dr. Smith when the latter asserts that God is participating in these processes and that "in principle there is but one truth about the whole religious life of mankind." [2] In any event, who can deny that the world religions are increasingly compelled to confront common problems, including the problems of secularization and secularism?

Considerations such as these move the present writer to indulge in contemplating a "rainbow of speculation." Looking toward the future we can envisage the possibility that a syncretism of some sort, along with new rivalries, new opportunities, and new problems, will emerge again in the development of Christianity and of other religions. In face of this sort of prognostication Troeltsch would perhaps be disposed to say again that "the great revelations of the various civilizations will remain distinct," though he would at the same time predict that "each racial group will strive to develop its own highest potentialities." But may not one also envisage the possibility that out of the new situation each of the religions will stimulate the others to conceive in new ways what is best in each of them?

These considerations suggest additional possibilities. On the one hand, some Christians may be expected to develop sufficient humility to recognize with H. Richard Niebuhr not only that the different religions ask fundamentally different questions but also that it is not mete for Christians to vaunt the alleged superiority of their norms, their obligation being rather to allow others peradventure to observe it. On the other hand, it is also possible that men will discover that Troeltsch was too "forcibly" impressed by the concept of individuality and that there are long-standing similarities and analogies between the high religions. Among others, Irving Babbitt a generation ago in the Introduction to his translation of *Dhammapada* (Oxford University Press, 1936) presented evidence of a common humanism in the norms of East and West. Is it not possible that a recognition of common elements in human nature will give rise to new, dynamic conceptions of the ethical doctrine of natural law? Actually, the study of the history of this doctrine and its variations engaged Troeltsch's attention for a long time. Nevertheless, in accord with the Historical School he allowed his sense of individuality in history to push the doctrine aside.

On the religious level, however, he maintained a tension within his mind, asserting on the one hand that "the divine life is not one but many" and on the other that "to apprehend the One in the many constitutes the special character of love." This paradox was for him "the icon of God."

All of these considerations attest the special relevance of the appearance now in English of Troeltsch's prophetic book of seventy years ago. In approaching our new situation we may say with Friedrich von Hügel that it is the merit of Troeltsch to help us grow in our very questions. In Troeltsch's view, precisely that process of growth should issue from "the specific kernel of religion," a unique and independent source of "new life and power."

—JAMES LUTHER ADAMS

---

[1] Wilhelm Pauck, *Harnack and Troeltsch* (New York: Oxford University Press, 1968), p. 68.

[2] "The Theology of Religions: Participation as a Possible Concept for a Theology of the Religious History of Mankind," a paper presented at the annual meeting of The American Theological Society, New York City, 1969.

TRANSLATOR'S NOTE

This translation involves unconventional renderings for several German terms, and it may be useful to some readers to know what those terms are. The following list is not exhaustive. It merely illustrates a few of the main problem areas. Terms are listed in approximately the order of their appearance in the text.

1. *Geschichte* and *Historie*: *Geschichte* generally refers to what happened in the past. It is practically synonymous with the English word "history." *Historie*, however, refers in this study to a particular outlook in terms of which history is regarded, understood, and written. Thus *die antike Historie*, for example, may be translated as "the understanding of history that prevailed in antiquity."

2. *Begriff*: The dictionary definition of *Begriff* is "concept," and in contemporary English usage the term "concept" ordinarily means a mental construct which may or may not correspond exactly to the reality one seeks to understand. In Troeltsch's hands, however, *Begriff* frequently involves a more objective reference than the English word "concept" does. The weight falls not so much on the mental image held by the thinker as on the reality that is in some sense external to the thinker. *Begriff* designates the metaphysical structure or principle of this reality. When so used, *Begriff* has generally been translated by the English word "principle."

3. *Prinzip*: The term *Prinzip* refers to the power or dynamic at work in a given reality. Since *Begriff* has first claim on the word "principle," *Prinzip* has usually been translated as "dynamic" or "dynamic principle."

4. *Kraft*: Though conventionally translated as "strength" or "power," Troeltsch often uses this term in the context of the history of religious development to refer to a religious idea or

principle that enters into history and, in the form of a particular religion, becomes a force in its own right. Since it is impossible to say all this in translating the word *Kraft,* it was decided to employ an English word which is admittedly less than perfect but which was deemed closer to the sense of the original than any of the dictionary definitions. This is the word "orientation." If orientation is understood not so much as something a person holds but more as an existing, living reality into which he enters, it may convey something of what Troeltsch was aiming at.

It should be remembered, however, that just as one German term may be translated into English in several different ways, so too, the same English word may refer to more than one term in the German. Oliver Wendell Holmes gave pungent expression to this point when he said, "A word is not a crystal transparent and unchanged; it is the skin of a living thought and may vary greatly in color and content according to the circumstances and the time in which it is used." Throughout, the translator's intention has been not to turn out a tortuously literal translation but to communicate in English idiom the cut and thrust of Troeltsch's argument.

It should be noted that the chapter titles do not occur in the German. At the suggestion of the publisher, they have been supplied by the translator.

The argument presented in this book is actually an expanded version of a lecture Troeltsch delivered in October 1901. Before that, he published an abstract of his lecture in the form of fourteen theses ("Thesen zu dem am 3. Oktober . . . zu haltenden Vortrage über *Die Absolutheit des Christentums und die Religionsgeschichte," Die Christliche Welt,* 15. Jahrgang, Nr. 39 [Sept. 26, 1901], cols. 923–925). As a result, he had the advantage of responses both to his abstract and to his lecture before he wrote the "Foreword to the First Edition." It may be suggested, therefore, that readers new to this book begin with the lecture itself and then come back to the "Foreword," which is essentially a dialogue with his contemporaries and presupposes some acquaintance with the substance of his argument.

Coaxing Troeltsch to express his rich, complex, and highly

purposive thought in readable English has not been a light task. If the result has any merit, it is due in large measure to the help I have received. Professor James Luther Adams, formerly of Harvard University and now a Distinguished Professor at Andover-Newton Theological School, encouraged this project from its inception and was instrumental in initiating arrangements to have it published by John Knox Press. Professor Roland Kircher, librarian of Wesley Theological Seminary in Washington, D. C., checked the first section of the translation at an early stage and helped me to comprehend more fully the intellectual milieu within which Troeltsch worked. To the Reverend Günter Dressler, a missionary of the Ost-Asia Mission now serving in Tokyo, I am particularly grateful for listening to every word of the translation in its first and literal stage while keeping the German text before him, and for helping me to make sense of difficult passages and gain a clearer understanding of nuances and emphases. Dr. Benjamin A. Reist, Professor of Systematic Theology at San Francisco Theological Seminary, most kindly studied the manuscript to make sure that the translation harmonizes with Troeltsch's work as a whole and that key philosophical and theological terms employed here to communicate Troeltsch's ideas correspond, as far as possible, to those now in use in American academic circles. Two close friends, Dr. I. John Hesselink, Professor of Church History and Ecclesiastical Latin at Tokyo Union Theological Seminary, and the Reverend David L. Swain, Associate Secretary of the Christian Scholars Fellowship (Japan) and of the Asia Committee of the World Student Christian Federation, read the translation through with particular attention to style and made many valuable criticisms and suggestions. Dr. Keith R. Crim, when he was book editor of John Knox Press, went beyond the call of duty by checking the translation against the German and suggesting ways to make the translation more accurate at certain points, more idiomatic at others. The present book editor, H. Davis Yeuell, very kindly accepted the responsibility of scouting out some bibliographical data for sources to which Troeltsch referred but for which he gave less information than is customary in American footnoting practice.

Many persons, therefore, have cooperated to make this work available to English readers, not least among them my wife, Etsu, whose helpfulness and good cheer often renewed a flagging or procrastinating spirit. I am profoundly grateful to all, though responsibility for the final form of this translation must of course remain my own.

Toward the end of his career, Troeltsch wrote an essay in which he passed in review some of his most important writings. The present book he spoke of as "the embryo for all that followed." Its importance for understanding the formative ideas of Troeltsch's thought has been evident for many years, and it may be that some of these ideas are not without significance, even today, for those who are concerned to think theologically about man and his religions. In any event the translator considers it a privilege to have had a hand in introducing, nearly seventy years after its first appearance, this remarkable little book which is regarded by many as a minor classic in the history of German theology.

DAVID REID

Japan Biblical Seminary
Tokyo, Japan

FOREWORD
TO THE
FIRST
EDITION

When I began to prepare this work for publication, it quickly outgrew the dimensions of a lecture, so I have abandoned the lecture form. The only reason I am retaining the designation of "lecture" is to show that this treatment of the problem originated in a request made to me and not in a desire on my part to respond to different approaches or to criticisms that appeared, no doubt fortuitously, during the summer of 1901. The lecture was promised before I learned of these works. However, I do not want to release it without making some brief comments about them at least in a foreword. In the body of the work itself I have limited myself to a discussion of essential principles.

In its main outlines Adolf von Harnack's rectorial address *Die Aufgabe der theologischen Fakultäten und die allgemeine Religionsgeschichte* [The Task of Theological Faculties and the General History of Religion] [1] deals with the same theme that this book does. On the whole I am in complete agreement with his main thesis. When it comes to particulars, however, my conception of and approach to the subject differ from his in certain respects as the following inquiry will show. To be specific, I find it impossible to hold that the consequence of modern studies and of views related to my own would be to change theological faculties into faculties for the study of the history of religion. I agree with Harnack that faculties of this kind would be utterly meaningless. What theology is concerned with is not the history of religion in general but *normative* knowledge acquired through the scientific study of religion. Only this can have meaning for theology. This normative knowledge is not one of many chimera-like possibilities that hover far off in the distance. It is within reach, and by a practical consensus among wide-ranging circles of influence in our present-day culture, it leads naturally in the direction of Christianity. What is important, therefore, in the first place, is to derive this normativeness from the history of religion instead of from scholastic theories of revelation or apologetics against philosophical systems, and then, in the second place, to give to the Christian world of thought a form that will correspond to the present religious and intellectual situation.

One who finds these endeavors frustrating and falls into an aimless relativism, or who believes that the goals of religion must be sought in some other direction, will of course have no desire to cooperate in the task of such a faculty. He who does cooperate, however, will attend to these matters at the time when he lays the foundation for his studies and life decisions, just as he will confront and make his decisions about those interpretations of the empirical world situation that indicate a basically antireligious tendency. But to build up a theological faculty that had no official knowledge of normative religious truth, that had to hunt for it like an explorer for the North Pole or a water witcher for water, would be a manifest absurdity. In religious matters he who would teach others must already have a position of his own and must be convinced that maintaining a position is a meaningful possibility. The possibility about which he is convinced, however, is not something infinitely remote, at least for the religious man, for religion has no meaning and indeed ceases to be religion if its truth and content are treated as something distant and supposedly quite unknown, if it is regarded as a source of eternally debatable problems rather than actually given divine actions and powers. It must be possible, without endless research, to achieve clarity as to this practical consensus of our life with respect to Christianity and, on the basis of such clarity, to cooperate with the scholarly institutions that serve the religious life of Christianity.

The nontheological scholar, as regards his attitude toward the religious problem, finds himself as a matter of course in substantially the same situation as the theologian or, more generally, in about the same situation as any well-educated man who reflects on these matters. But since his educational work serves neither religious understanding nor the furthering of the religious life, he is not bound, as the theologian is, to have attained a relatively sure standpoint as a presupposition of his educational work. If he so desires and if circumstances permit, he can leave the matter open permanently. But the scholars who belong to theological faculties are by nature committed to some definite point of view that has to be acquired before they begin their educational work.

However, the process of thought that leads to this point of view and the theological theories that develop it are not thus bound. Such thought must of course begin by treating this viewpoint as something that is hypothetically to be called into question. On the basis of general considerations, it infers as result that which was once seriously doubted and which was first permanently adopted because of comprehensive reflections based on principle. For the educated man in the present intellectual climate this is unavoidable. All this relates, however, only to the basic question of the normative validity of Christianity. Questions of a more specific nature are of course not disposed of at so basic a level but must remain open problems for the work of a theological faculty. But this basic question has to be settled first, and it will be more easily settled if theology, as a result of reflections and decisions on this fundamental matter, is successful in constructing a theory that emphasizes what is important and thus simplifies the problem. To provide a theory that will serve those who are struggling with this fundamental decision, and by means of this theory to prepare the way for subsequent detailed studies that do not presuppose a particular point of view—that is the main purpose of this work. However, such a theory must, in my opinion, go into the general history of religion more thoroughly than Harnack appears inclined to allow, though I share his view that the history of religion is only a presuppositional and auxiliary discipline as far as theology is concerned. I approach the problem from the perspective of the systematic theologian, who has to grasp and dispose of presuppositions in the most radical way, while he speaks from the perspective of the church historian, who is inclined, rather, to consider them as already disposed of and therefore defines the problem more narrowly.

The second theological and rectorial address of the year that came into my hands after this work had been completed was Adolf Jülicher's *Moderne Meinungsverschiedenheiten über Methoden, Aufgaben und Ziele der Kirchengeschichte* [Contemporary Differences of Opinion as to the Methods, Tasks, and Goals of Church History],[2] which is also concerned with the subject of this inquiry. Yet even though he makes unmistakable allusions to some of my ideas, I think I should not regard his address as referring to me, for Jülicher's arguments depend on an interpretation of my short essay "Ueber historische und dogmatische Methode in der Theologie" [The Historical vs. the Dogmatic Method in Theology] that is in many ways precluded by my earlier works. Moreover, as far as substance is concerned, I cannot make sense of his strangely complicated denial of my proposals except in terms of the idea that is developed, after further reflection on the problem, in the present work.

Perhaps I should have emphasized more strongly the distinction between the study of history itself and the philosophical reflection upon history that derives from it. This philosophical reflection is, however, a result that arises directly out of the study of history, and it is a result that Jülicher himself does not avoid when he says that he has "no more intention of ruling out value judgments than of ruling out the endeavor to place isolated events in a context and see individual phenomena whole in the living flow of a highly complex development" (p. 13). Nor does he avoid this result when he says: "Just place Christianity and its churches among the other religions and it will be splendidly vindicated" (p. 15). My opinion is precisely the same. I believe, however, that these ultimately decisive ideas that condition one's attitude toward the whole ought not to remain in the form of occasional aphorisms by church historians but that these seeds should be developed into a theory in which such a view, together with its presuppositions and consequences, will be thought out on principle. In so doing, one cannot proceed without "effusions of philosophy of religion" and precarious generalizations. But what I am most concerned with is to provide a basis in principle for the approach we make to this subject. This is suggested, as a matter of fact, in the works of this same prominent scholar. Jülicher himself speaks of "the idea, borrowed from another world view, of an exclusive antithesis between the natural and the religious man." A world view opposed to this one, however, can only be one that grows out of the study of history with its substitution of relative antitheses for absolute ones. It is precisely at this point that it is necessary to think through these antitheses in terms of their normative meaning and of the effect they have on our way of thinking about Christianity.

Turning now to important older statements, insofar as the well-known book by C. A. Bernoulli, *Die wissenschaftliche und die kirchliche Methode in der Theologie* [The Scientific Method and the Ecclesiastical Method in Theology],[3] represents ideas leading in the same direction as my own, I find myself obliged to concur with him also. Nevertheless, I believe that Bernoulli considerably overestimates the effects of historical relativism and that the whole problem can be treated in a much calmer frame of mind. A scientifically informed theology that makes the very foundation of Christianity into an insoluble problem for the foreseeable future is its own undoing and is, in my judgment, an unfortunate exaggeration of the results of a scientific approach to religion. Moreover, the ecclesiastical theology to which it gives rise must accordingly meet with derision and lose all foundation. Therefore, as regards the theology of institutional Christianity, there is only one point I can admit as justified: In view of the great change in the traditional understanding of Christianity due to the emergence of a theology grounded in the history of religion, a cautious, careful, and sensitively reforming accommodation is necessary in the training of seminarians, particularly in the theological instruction of those who desire to serve a church for which there is definite historical authority. For the rest I refer the reader to my review of this interesting book in

the *Göttingische gelehrte Anzeigen*, 160. Jahrgang (1898), 425–
435. I regard Wilhelm Herrmann's dogmatic theology as a master-
piece of such accommodation. To be sure, it is not intended as
such, but like all dogmatic theologies, it is so, which is to say that
it involves accommodation on a grand scale.

From the ranks of the Ritschlian school three essays have
appeared: (1) Georg Wobbermin, "Das Verhältnis der Theologie
zur modernen Wissenschaft und ihre Stellung im Gesamtrahmen
der Wissenschaften" [The Relationship of Theology to Modern
Science and Its Position in the Framework of the Sciences as a
Whole]; [4] (2) Friedrich Traub, "Die religionsgeschichtliche Methode und die systematische Theologie" [The Method of the History of Religion and Systematic Theology]; [5] and (3) Max
Reischle, "Historische und dogmatische Methode der Theologie"
[Historical and Dogmatic Method in Theology].[6] Their main
objections are partially met by the ideas developed in this book.
In part, however, I must stand by what I have said before. Despite various points of agreement, here one conception in its
entirety is set over against another.

When I designated my approach *in toto* as a "historical"
method in contrast to the dogmatic, I realized that this historical
method could be so named only *a parte portiori*, only from the
point of view of antithesis. The historical method involves a
comprehensive perspective based on the breadth of the historical
and developed from the concepts of universality formed thereby.
It represents an attempt to work out the unique character of
historical conceptualization in distinction both from the kind of
conceptualization that takes place in the natural sciences and
from speculative universal concepts that disregard the differentiation between the former two. It seeks thereby to free historical
conceptualization from the difficulties that have always smothered
the latter two when they were really applied to the study of
history. The historical method must be conceived in such a way
that what is relative and individual in history will come into its
own as a factor that dominates history unconditionally. Yet it
must also be conceived in such a way as not to exclude from
these individual and relative phenomena the emergence of au-

thentic values which, in consequence of their validity, are directed toward a common goal.

I have also realized that this way of thinking about history and this attempt to derive the normative from the study of history render impossible the purely phenomenological and causal view of history and human events that is demanded by Kantian doctrine, on the one hand, and even more emphatically by neo-Kantian doctrine, on the other, with its setting aside of freedom and the practical reason. I have neither sought to demonstrate on behalf of religion generally gaps in the causal view into which supernatural influences might be inserted, as Reischle thinks, nor confused causal explanation with a valuational way of looking at things, as Traub supposes. Instead, I contest the universal applicability of the causal view, in the sense of a closed system of necessary causes and effects, as far as historical phenomena and the entire compass of human events are concerned. (Cf., in this regard, my criticism of R. A. Lipsius' *Lehrbuch der evangelisch-protestantischen Dogmatik* [Manual of Protestant Dogmatic Theology], 3. Aufl.,[7] published in the *Göttingische gelehrte Anzeigen*, 156. Jahrgang [1894], 841–854.) I do this not merely because a purely causal-mechanistic view and a valuational one simply cannot be left as parallels that never meet, but also because I have never been able to convince myself that the causal approach, starting from perceptions and desires and ending up with ideas and universal values, can really prove feasible. Further, I think that the entire life of the human spirit, in its relation to an intangible reality, requires an ontological foundation in principles independent of those appropriate to the causal-mechanistic approach. The entire doctrine of a purely causal, yet also purely phenomenal, occurrence of all the manifestations of consciousness seems to me an illegitimate and unconfirmed transposing of the doctrine of "external experience" into one of "internal experience."

These problems are in any event exceedingly complicated. To contest the application of a mechanizing view of causality to every sphere of human life may, in addition to being a theological heresy, also be a philosophical one; or it may be that my attempt to demonstrate this point will be judged a failure. I maintain, however, that it is inadmissible to identify science with causal explanation, and that where such identification occurs, there is no room for religion in the real meaning of the word. I would go so far as to say that the Kantian doctrine of intelligible character and of motivation through the purely rational necessity of the good, and in particular Kant's philosophy of history, with its depiction of the development of a realm of moral reason, has broken through the rigidity of a purely phenomenological and causal view and made use of an ontological approach to human events. At any rate I regard it as essential to place the scientifically oriented appraisal of religion on a broad foundation by demonstrating the truth of such an ontological principle, and to answer the question as to the normative development of religion on the basis of a conceptual analysis of the higher types of religious life that appear in history.

The neo-Kantian theologians, who oppose this latter point so strenuously, are in any case unable to unite their own doctrine of the absolute validity of historical Christianity, which hinges on the impression made by the historical Christ, with their neo-Kantian principles. According to these principles, every particular event in history, including both the man Jesus and Christianity itself, belongs to a causal-mechanical phenomenological stratum, while the only thing that transcends history is universally valid, rationally necessary moral judgment. This implication cannot be refuted by asserting that Kant's sense of history, along with that of the entire eighteenth century, is to be condemned, for Kant as a matter of fact was by no means devoid of a sense of history. In his case, however, even a most refined sense of history availed nothing against the implications of his phenomenological theory of causality. I have always found that it is not a sense of history that frees the neo-Kantian theologian from the constraints of these implications. What frees him is, rather, a highly fragile link between, on the one hand, a view of history as tradition in which Christianity is dogmatically isolated from its connections with its environment, and, on the other hand, serious and critical historical studies, ethical postulates, and apologetic references to claims of a morally pure man—claims that, if they are not true, must be fraudulent or delusory. A sense of history seems to me, however, to demand something essentially different, and it is this different conception that I have attempted to set forth in the present book.

In its denial of the neo-Kantianizing view of religion and its demand for the acknowledgment of ontological principles, the careful and instructive essay by Ludwig Ihmels, *Die Selbständigkeit der Dogmatik gegenüber der Religionsphilosophie* [The Independence of Dogmatic Theology in Distinction from the Philosophy of Religion] [8] in the Erlangen presentation volume dedicated to His Royal Highness the Prince Regent in 1901, is in harmony with my approach. For this reason the author criticizes my studies not only with understanding but even, in part, with sympathy. He objects, however, that no one who starts from my position can arrive at an attitude toward Christianity that will be characterized by joy and certainty. He maintains that securing such an attitude requires that the position taken toward Christianity be derived strictly from an inquiry concerned with Christianity alone as a definitely given object, excluding consideration of any other religions—thus by a *Christian* epistemology developed on the basis of this object. Such a Christian epistemology can by nature and with complete certainty base its valuation of this object exclusively upon the unique, supernatural, miraculous causality of the experience of conversion through which the Bible acts upon men and through which the Bible is at the same time authenticated.

The reply to be made to this view is that the certainty to which Ihmels aspires is attained only by means of the supernatural factor he introduces, a factor that isolates Christianity absolutely from other historical phenomena. But even a purely formal restricting of the problem of certainty to Christianity must, for its part, hypothetically treat its object as a problem in the same way this inquiry does. It must first consider psychologically and historically the religious experience that affirms Christianity. Here too, since it is a scientific investigation, the result must be left open, just as I have done. The inquiry that

Ihmels proposes is merely simpler and concerned with fewer interrelational structures than mine. From his standpoint, however, complete certainty can be acquired only by reference to the supernatural principle that is first apprehended in inner miracle and is then, on that basis, corroborated by external miracle. In opposition to the modern study of history, reference is then made to the point that history cannot prove the impossibility of miracle and, being a secular discipline, is unable to get at the religious meaning that of itself guarantees the reality of miracle. What is decisive, in my judgment, is not the fact of starting from an isolated object as the only object that is really known to us, but the discovery of completely unique and miraculous causality in this object. This discovery is of course made much easier by the refusal to take historical comparison between religions as a point of departure.

Ihmels' fundamental objection to my approach is that it does not attain supernatural certainty. This certainty, however, seems unattainable to me because the relative, historical, and limited character of the history of Christian development has been established, in my view, by proofs whose validity cannot be diminished either by the abstract impossibility of the denial of miracle or by the postulates of a religious orientation. The inquiry, for this reason, does indeed become more complicated, and its result remains without the certainty that miracle gives—though as I hope to have shown in what follows, it does not remain without the certainty that faith gives. But the method by which this result is obtained should not be confronted with the dilemma that certainty has to be derived either through "logical argument from the philosophy of religion or through religious experience." Ihmels contends that the former already presupposes the latter in the form of an affirmation of a definite religion. He holds that the Christian, despite his comparison of Christianity with other religions, always remains bound to an affirmation of his own that is specifically grounded in Christianity. The Christian theologian, therefore, might just as well either have done with all this comparing and contrasting or engage in it after adopting a definite point of view. In short, all philosophy of religion depends, according to Ihmels, on a self-deception in which a person takes what is known to him alone, something innate and unique, and places it on a false foundation instead of acknowledging a unique basis of certainty.

The way Ihmels argues here, however, constitutes a dangerous apologetic. It would have the result of confining every man to the religion in which he was born and would make religious conviction into *une affaire de géographie,* as Rousseau held, though it is true that those born within Christianity would thus be in a more advantageous situation for discovering the supernatural factor.

Granted, an inquiry based on philosophy of religion does presuppose religious experience, but not in the form of the abrupt either/or with which the dogmatic and supernaturalistic way of thinking has made us familiar. The essence of the modern approach to history is hypothetical and sympathetic understanding. By virtue of this approach it is possible for one to understand modes of religious life other than his own, on the one hand, and to objectify his own religious orientation hypothetically, on the other. This is to say that he can call into question any simple, exclusive valuation of the religion to which he belongs. Inquiry oriented to the philosophy of religion does rest on experience—not, however, on a unique, isolated experience but on one that has numerous aspects. It rests not on a singular experience that is dogmatically affirmed but on one that has many facets, that embraces other persons and groups, and that is capable of being understood hypothetically and sympathetically. The final decision between the values thus apprehended is, to be sure, ultimately an axiomatic act. The motives of this act, however, are made clear through an examination and gradation of the values compared and hence through bringing them into relation with what they hold in common. To aim the pistol of the either/or at a person is typical of the dogmatic method, while a contextual consideration of the both/and is characteristic of the historical. Of these two, it is the latter, understood in the sense of philosophy of history, that is important here.

To me, the most significant thing about the historical method is not only that in this way the attaining of Christian certainty will be placed on a broader and conceptually more universal basis. It is that this kind of viewpoint is the only one in which detailed historical research into the Christian religion will not be bound to prejudgments. Conversely, the ultimate result of Ihmels' way of undergirding certainty is to clinch more tightly judgments that have already been made in advance.

If the essay by Ihmels is a model of distinguished, conscientious, and instructive polemics, then the rejoinder that Heinrici has ventured to publish under the sensational title *Dürfen wir noch Christen bleiben?* [Can We Still Be Christians?] [9] is characterized by vagueness and superficiality. After a cursory reference to Lagarde, Heinrici here associates me with Darwin and Strauss. He imputes to me a "naturalistic" doctrine of evolution that applies natural causality to personal life and that knows neither the significance of the great geniuses for the study of history nor absolute values or goals of the inner life! He brushes aside my major essays, in which the doctrine of evolution is cautiously interpreted and the intervention of natural causality explicitly ruled out, with the flippant comment that I, "after a few vacillations," have finally made my teaching conveniently available in the short essay "Ueber historische und dogmatische Methode in der Theologie"—though the fact is that this essay has as its presupposition everything I had written before. Ihmels even seems to suggest that he, in contrast to me, regards Wellhausen and Fechner as tolerable Christians. Yet in my lengthy article "Die Selbständigkeit der Religion" [The Independence of Religion],[10] I made frequent and express reference to Fechner's excellent book *Die drei Motive und Gründe des Glaubens* [The Three Motives and Grounds of Faith],[11] while as for Wellhausen's method of research, I have gone on record as saying that my essay was an attempt to translate that method into a theory.[12]

Nothing of value is to be expected from a careless polemic of this kind. Moreover, even Heinrici's positive ideas can be turned to no good account, since they cannot be disentangled from the jumble of ambiguous distortions and insinuations. But one point is clear, and that I want to stress, because this is a point I have always found particularly objectionable, Heinrici presenting a characteristic example of what I emphatically dispute.

Heinrici himself adheres to the historical way of thinking and has for his own part most meritoriously enriched it through his demonstration of continuities between the structure of the primitive Christian fellowship and the currents of the classical world and its society. But all inconvenient consequences of thinking historically about Christianity he snips off at the point where they pinch, saying that he regards them as "results of conceiving the problem incorrectly" (p. 3). "Nowhere do false formulations of the problem engender more confusion than in the religious sphere." Certainly! That is the trouble with a theology that mixes up historical and dogmatic ways of thinking. It allows the greatest latitude to the scientific study of history in general, but wherever such study opposes the traditional view too strongly, suddenly this theology is prepared with special formulations of the problem, formulations of a theological kind. Heinrici has also instructively pointed out the secret of this problem-formulation and its marvelous effects by showing that in problems involving Christianity the following presuppositions must always be included: (1) Christianity is to be regarded exclusively as an individual historical phenomenon in the light of its claim to unique and absolute truth. In this way the dogmatic-apologetic image of Christianity is without further ado identified with the phenomenon itself. (2) Everything that is not directly and absolutely refutable by the historical critic (and when such cases arise, the standards the critic must meet are taken very strictly) must be regarded by theology as possible, and this is a specific theological principle. (3) The assertions of Biblical history concerning the traditions that attest its miraculous character—assertions thus regarded as possible, or at least irrefutable—are to be considered as positive truths when the concept of a universal essence or principle of religion is taken into account along with its postulate of absolutely supernatural realization. Thus quite specific theological results are expected from this concept of a universal principle of religion.

This formulation of problems involves, then, an underlying

"world view" that is nowhere supported by argument and developed as such. Instead, it always remains enveloped in hazy formulations of this kind, yet it is opposed to the allegedly naturalistic world view on the basis of which I am said to operate. With the proviso that the presuppositions specified above be employed, Christianity is to be investigated historically, impartially, and with full recourse to otherwise valid historical methods! Surely, however, this is to pose problems as if they were mousetraps, and one can hardly blame outsiders if theology appears to them as a tainted discipline. This means that the important question is entirely circumvented, namely, whether historical inquiry, quite of itself and without any connection with world views and the like, has not rendered impossible any conception of the history of primitive Christianity that would support an approach of this kind.

Heinrici's approach, moreover, leaves unexamined the fundamental presupposition upon which all else depends, namely, the presupposition of a specific and exclusive supernaturalism. This presupposition, incidentally, is by no means identical with theism, with recognition of the absolute goals of personal life, or with appreciation for the significance of the underivable and original revelations of human creativity in the great geniuses. To all these I too lay claim; the antithesis occurs within the sphere marked out by these ideas. Thus everything remains obscure, and more exact discussion is impossible. I am content, therefore, to reply to the malicious question Heinrici used for a title with a less harmful counterquestion. This question likewise implies its own answer and therefore, on Heinrici's terms, constitutes a theologically correct formulation of the problem. The question is this: What should those who sit in glass houses, even if those houses are in a relatively sheltered place, not throw?

After so many distortions and contradictions, it gives me special pleasure to refer to the new book by Rudolf Eucken, *Der Wahrheitsgehalt der Religion* [The Truth of Religion].[13] At most points the views expressed in this book coincide with mine, and above all, its overall conception is closely related to my own. Whoever reads this work will discover that I have learned much from its author, though in passing I would like to emphasize the point that our agreement in matters of major importance is a result of work we carried out independently.

My critics have often reproached me with overestimating the newness of my theory. I cannot concur in this opinion, for I have constantly held that this theory is concerned with problems of long standing, problems that were never adequately considered and that were resolved in appearance only. That I am aware of the age of these problems may be shown, in conclusion, by referring to two older sources that give characteristic formulation to the motive that has led me to the present work.

Kant once wrote to Johann Georg Hamann with reference to Herder's *Älteste Urkunde des Menschengeschlechts* [The Earliest Document of the Human Race]:

> When a religion is once so organized that critical knowledge of ancient languages and erudition in philology and ancient documents constitute the foundation upon which it must be erected in all ages and among all peoples, then he who is most skilled in Greek, Hebrew, Syriac, Arabic, and the like, and thus in the archives of antiquity, will drag the orthodox about anywhere as if they were children; they may not put up the slightest resistance, for by their own protestation they cannot match themselves against one who possesses such authority, so they timidly look on and see how a Michael melts down their ancient treasure and gives it an entirely different stamp. If theological faculties were gradually to de-emphasize the requirement of having seminary students persevere at this kind of (historical) literature, as at least appears to be the case among us, and if freethinking philologists alone were to make themselves the masters of these formidable weapons, then the reputation of the orthodox leaders of the people would be entirely at an end. For whatever they teach *they would have to obtain the instruction of the literati* . . . and these in turn would not easily allow the unconsecrated to carry this prize away from their territory.[14]

This observation is particularly appropriate to the present day, when theological faculties are under pressure from church-related political parties and when free inquiry into primitive Christianity is increasingly, and again to a remarkable degree, being taken over by the philologists.

If, however, one puts forward the objection that in historical phenomena religious values arise that are not identical with the phenomena themselves and that are to be affirmed from a practical point of view, then what Schleiermacher once said holds good:

> A desire for the manifestation of the spirit that has not yet appeared necessarily presupposes a likeness between the spirit in the universally human sense—for only in this spirit could the desire exist—and the πνεῦμα, the divine and dynamic principle of Christianity. Likeness, however, is inconceivable without unity between the members, which here means identity between the spirit in the universally human sense and the spirit in the Christian sense. It appears, therefore, that we have come close to the so-called rational view of Christianity, according to which the πνεῦμα of Christ is identical with the spirit in the universally human sense, though in a higher form. However, we can equally well set forth this proposition: "It must be presupposed that both are identical; hence *the spirit in the universal human sense is exactly what the πνεῦμα is,* but it is that πνεῦμα at a lower power." And as soon as we say, as we now do, that this lower power is incapable of being raised up to the higher in and of itself, then we have joined together what seemed to be rationalistic and what seemed to be supernatural. The difference between the two is nullified, a result at which one always and necessarily arrives if he pursues the antithesis to its conclusion.[15]

If Kant's words show us what the eighteenth century perceived above all else, namely, the multiplicity and conditionality of everything historical in antithesis to the demand for unconditioned truths, Schleiermacher exhibits the attempt of German idealism to overcome this historical relativity by a way other than that of ahistorical rationalism, namely, by ontological speculation concerning history—speculation that, through reflection on the very multiplicity of history, leads to knowledge of the unitary ground of all life.

It is by way of this path, I believe, that our work must ultimately proceed, even though Schleiermacher's position is definitely not the last word on the subject. On the contrary, the modern study of history confronts this position with even more difficult problems, for it is no longer possible, with Schleiermacher, to confine to Christianity alone the rise of the spirit to a higher power; it is equally impossible to construe Christianity— even if limited to the person of Jesus alone—as the absolute, history-transcending realization of the spirit. In this regard the tendency indicated in Kant's observations has proved itself only too powerful. At this point, however, Schleiermacher has already indicated the precariousness of his position. This precariousness is due to his artificial combining of reflections derived from the philosophy of religion with the self-attestation of the Christian community, a combination rightly perceived by Ihmels as particularly difficult.[16] To discuss these difficulties anew and, if possible, to overcome them without such a cleverly balanced dialectic is the concern of the present work.

FOREWORD
TO THE
SECOND
EDITION

The present work has been out of print for some time. With this new edition I have been obliged to choose whether to rework it entirely and incorporate it into a still more comprehensive frame of thought, or to let it go essentially unchanged. I have decided on the latter course, partly because of lack of time at the moment, and partly because the book belongs, in the last analysis, to a definite situation in the theological consideration of the problem and is indissolubly bound up with it. The situation is no longer quite the same today. The problems raised in the last decade have become far more acute. For those who make the situation of that time their starting point, however, this book may be of some service in facilitating an understanding of the shifts that have subsequently taken place.

Besides a number of reviews—among which I would like to draw particular attention to those by Wilhelm Herrmann,[1] Paul Jäger,[2] and Rudolf Eucken[3]—this book has occasioned a variety of responses that I can only catalogue here: Thomä, *Die Absolutheit des Christentums* [The Absoluteness of Christianity];[4] Brunstäd, *Ueber die Absolutheit des Christentums* [On the Absoluteness of Christianity];[5] Beth, "Das Wesen des Christentums und die historische Forschung" [The Essence of Christianity and Historical Inquiry][6] (the author, as a result of studies in biology, has now changed his outlook); Heinrici, *Theologie und Religionswissenschaft* [Theology and the Scientific Study of Religion][7] (the author, in distinction from his earlier work, here aspires to complete impartiality); Hunzinger, "Die religionsphilosophische Aufgabe der kirchlichen Theologie" [The Task of Theology in

the Area of Philosophy of Religion] [8] and *Probleme und Auf-
gaben der gegenwärtigen systematischen Theologie* [Problems
and Tasks of Contemporary Systematic Theology]; [9] Ludwig
Ihmels, "Blicke in die neuere dogmatische Arbeit" [Glances at
More Recent Works in Dogmatic Theology]; [10] Wilhelm Bousset,
"Kantisch-Friessche Religionsphilosophie und ihre Anwendung
auf die Theologie" [Kantian-Friesian Philosophy of Religion and
Its Application to Theology].[11] Also worthy of mention here are
E. Spranger, *Die Grundlagen der Geschichtswissenschaft* [Founda-
tions of the Scientific Study of History],[12] and most recently Theo-
dor Kaftan, *Ernst Troeltsch, eine kritische Zeitstudie* [Ernst
Troeltsch, a Critical Study of His Thought in Terms of His
Milieu],[13] which in form is an exemplary polemical treatise.
Writings that agree with and appropriate the standpoint repre-
sented here are fewer in number. In certain respects Eucken's
Hauptprobleme der Religionsphilosophie der Gegenwart [Key
Problems in the Philosophy of Religion Today] [14] and possibly
Wernle's well-known *Einführung in das theologische Studium*
[Introduction to the Study of Theology] [15] may be included
under this heading.

A discussion of these differing expressions of opinion is not
possible here. I must defer such a discussion to a carefully worked-
out philosophy of religion, which will be my next task. Here I
should simply like to point out that by virtue of all these discussions, the problem can be seen very clearly indeed. One group of
writers is troubled by the absence of miracle, which I am admittedly not prepared to acknowledge as a uniquely Christian
causality. Yet with regard to the radical rationalism of universal
law, which many secretly suspect me of, I venture to refer to my
essay on "Die Bedeutung des Begriffes der Kontingenz" [The
Meaning of the Concept of Contingency].[16] The basic idea of
this essay was already part of my thinking at the time the present
book was written. To another group the emphasis on historical
and positive elements as over against the "idea" is insufficient.
To still others this emphasis is, conversely, too strong, and they
think they find at this point an irremediable flaw in my reasoning.
All in all, my position and the problems it involves are indeed

well described. I propose, however, to continue maintaining this position and hope to be able to provide it with even more comprehensive foundations.

Some readers might like to have an indication of where I have treated some of the problems connected with this position. The problem of mission I took up in "Die Mission in der modernen Welt" [Mission in the Modern World],[17] as well as in an essay written to clarify this article entitled "Missionsmotiv, Missionsaufgabe und neuzeitliches Humanitätschristentum" [The Motive and Task of Mission and a Modern Christianity that Regards Man Contextually],[18] which was a reply to Gustav Warneck. In the little book *Die Bedeutung der Geschichtlichkeit Jesu für den Glauben* [The Significance of the Historicity of Jesus for Faith],[19] I have described the attitude toward the person of Jesus which results from this position, and I have clarified the relation between this approach and the spirit and instincts of institutional Christianity in *Soziallehren der christlichen Kirchen und Gruppen* [Social Teachings of the Christian Churches and Groups].[20] Finally, examples of how dogmatic themes would be treated on the basis of this position are contained for the present in the first edition of the theological encyclopedia *Religion in Geschichte und Gegenwart.*

The few changes in this new edition are merely stylistic. I have eliminated a few of the stylistically crude sentences for which Herrmann rightly reproved me. Also, the more recent literature has been taken into consideration as far as it is known to me. For the rest, the overly terse text was made somewhat clearer and expanded in a few places.

ERNST TROELTSCH

Heidelberg
December 1, 1911

This third edition is an unaltered reprint of the second, though a few glaring typographical errors have been corrected.

1

BACKGROUND
OF THE
PROBLEM
OF THE
ABSOLUTENESS
OF
CHRISTIANITY

It may be taken for granted that the modern world, in the great and dominating forms it has assumed since the eighteenth century, represents a unique type of culture. As such, it stands in contrast to the culture of antiquity and to medieval Catholic culture, from the latter of which the culture of early Protestant orthodoxy did not make an altogether clean break. One of the most important characteristics of this new world is the development of an unreservedly historical view of human affairs.

The modern idea of history is a dynamic principle for attaining a comprehensive view of everything human. It grew originally out of the Enlightenment and its criticism of political and social institutions, out of the Reformation and its battle against Catholic tradition, and out of the renewal of Christian and classical philology. It was given added depth by the great world views of the period of German idealism, especially those views relating to the history of evolution. Eventually it grew from isolated monographs into an independent discipline which, in connection with the object of its study, has developed into a unique mode of thought and research that has authenticated itself with most brilliant results. The more this idea of history has been emancipated from extraneous metaphysical prejudgments and gained recognition as a way of thinking independent of the formulation of concepts that takes place in the natural sciences, the more it has demonstrated that it is the matrix out of which all world views take shape.[1]

This does not mean that the modern idea of history merely puts greater emphasis on ways of looking at things that were also employed earlier. It is something new in principle, a consequence of an expanding of men's horizons both backward into the past and laterally across the entire breadth of the present. As a result, the original naïve certainty held by every existing type of culture and value system regarding the obviousness of its own validity has been shaken. Each culture, each value system, is treated as one object of historical investigation among others, and through comparison between such objects it has now become possible, for the first time, to arrive at criteria of value. Thus the modern idea of history marks the end of dogmatic conceptualization which hypostatizes naïve claims to validity with a few comparatively simple notions such as revelations or truths of natural reason. The modern idea of history, that is to say, is in principle a new mode of thought that gains its orientation from history itself.

The understanding of history that prevailed in antiquity was the history of single states. It operated with the rudiments of historical criticism, with excellent but fragmentary results in terms of analogical and psychological comprehension, and with political and patriotic criteria. The idea of history in Catholic culture was the history of mankind. It proceeded, however, not only with purely dogmatic criteria used to absolutize the classical culture of Catholicism but also with a commitment to subordinate all important matters to purely dogmatic postulates. Thus it drew everything together under one all-embracing critique that involved an almost total absence of skill in, or inclination toward, sympathetic understanding. In both cases the idea of history was an appendix or adjunct to the dominant thought of the culture. It conformed to the national, rational, or theological norms of thought.

In contrast to these two ways of thinking, the modern idea of history, which depends on critical source-analysis and on conclusions derived from psychological analogy, is the history of the development of peoples, spheres of culture, and cultural components. It dissolves all dogmas in the flow of events and tries sympathetically to do justice to all phenomena, first measuring them by their own criteria and then combining them into an overall picture of the continuous and mutually conditioning factors in all individual phenomena that shape the unfolding development of mankind. This overall picture, steadily pursued despite the incompleteness and uncertainty of our knowledge, is today, with all its different stages of development, the presupposition of every judgment concerning the norms and ideals of mankind. For this reason the modern idea of history is no longer merely one aspect of a way of looking at things or a partial satisfaction of the impetus to knowledge. It is, rather, the foundation of all thinking concerning values and norms. It is the medium for the self-reflection of the species upon its nature, origins, and hopes.

It is easy to see how Christianity is affected by this mode of thought which is entirely free as regards the outcome of specific investigations and yet bound to definite methodological presuppositions. Christianity, like all great religious movements, has from the outset possessed a naïve certainty as to its normative truth. Apologetic reflections have fortified this confidence since the earliest times by contrasting Christianity with everything non-Christian as a whole. In this way the latter became more and more a homogeneous mass of human error while the former became more and more a divinely ordained institution, recognizable as such on the basis of external and internal miracle. Ecclesiastical philosophy and theology then perfected the concept of the church. Founded as an absolute miracle and authenticating itself in the miracles of conversion and the sacraments, the church was conceived as a supernatural institution that stands within history but does not derive from history. Ordinary history with its merely human and humanly conditioned truths is, according to this view, the sphere of sin and error. Only history as written by the church gives truth that is absolutely certain, though not absolutely exhaustive, because it works with powers that derive not from history but directly from God.

The modern idea of history, however, has had a radically

dissolving effect on this apologetic structure of thought. Opposition to the rationalistic watering down of Christianity, often thought of as a kind of restoration of church-oriented theology, led to a revival of the notion of the historical uniqueness of Christianity. But this in turn simply led to the incorporation of Christianity as one individual phenomenon into the current of the other great individual phenomena that history has brought forth, even though the Christian phenomenon was not to be declared false on the basis of extraneous normative concepts. In particular it led to the incorporating of Christianity into the context of the history of religions. The apologetic wall of division, the wall of external and internal miracle, has slowly been broken down by this idea of history, for no matter what one may otherwise think about miracles, it is impossible for historical thought to believe the Christian miracles but deny the non-Christian. Again, however frequently one may discern something supernatural in the ethical power of the inner life, no means exist by which to construe the Christian's elevation above sensuality as supernatural while interpreting that of Plato or Epictetus as natural. With this, however, there no longer exists any means by which one may isolate Christianity from the rest of history and then, on the basis of this isolation and its formal signs, define it as an absolute norm. This impossibility is made even more acute by the fact that Christianity, as far as its content is concerned, presents itself as a mere fragment of divine truth and thus knows that it can bring forth only humanly incomplete results.

Viewed positively, however, every step that establishes connections between early Christian history and pre- or extra-Christian phenomena, every discovery of similarity between Christianity and other objects of investigation as a result of critical research into sources and traditions, every application of contemporary psychological methods of observation to religion and to the development of religious concepts, signifies a victory in the illumination of this magnificent historical phenomenon. This is what justifies a skeptical outlook that opposes the various means by which Christianity has been isolated from other human history—means that have been used, and are used even today in apologetic theology, to demonstrate the normative truth of Christianity solely out of its own resources without a single glance at other history.

Once the modern idea of history made it impossible to prove the normative value of Christian thought by the means the church had traditionally used, attempts were made to reach the goal by yet another path. Its starting point was the concept of a total history of mankind, with history taken as a dynamic principle in its own right. The history of mankind was viewed causally and teleologically as a single whole. Within this whole the ideal of religious truth was thought of as moving forward in gradual stages, and at one definite point, namely, in the historical phenomenon of Christianity, it was deemed to have reached absolute form, i.e., the complete and exhaustive realization of its principle.

This approach remained true to the Enlightenment and its incorporating of Christianity into the religions of the world. It also remained true to the historico-critical way of viewing Christianity. Because the totality of history in general and the history of religion in particular were comprehended by an all-embracing intuition and were brilliantly interpreted, it was expected that this approach would overcome the tension between the multiplicity of history and its relative, individual forms. It was to do so by means of the concept of a universal principle that bore within itself the law of its movement from lower, obscure, and embryonic beginnings to complete, clear, and conscious maturity—a universal principle represented as a normative power actualizing itself by degrees in the course of history. In this way Christianity was held up as the actualization of the principle of religion, the absolute religion in antithesis to mediated and veiled expressions of this principle. There exists, in reality, only *one* religion, namely, the principle or essence of religion, and this principle of religion, this essence of religion, is latent in all historical religions as their ground and goal. In Christianity this universally latent essence, everywhere else limited by its media, has appeared in untrammeled and exhaustive perfection. If Christianity is thus identical with this principle of religion that is elsewhere implicit and that comes to complete explication only in Christianity, then the Christian religion is of course normative religious truth. Thus the older apologetic speculation, which opposed history, has been replaced by a new one that is on the side of history. Thus too, in fact, the concept of a principle of Christianity that is at the same time the realization of the principle of religion as such has become the foundation of the modern apologetic.

After Lessing's, Kant's, and Herder's philosophies of history had prepared the way for this view, two leaders of German idealism who are at the same time the fathers of the new historico-critical and yet religion-affirming theology (Schleiermacher and Hegel) took this conceptual framework and in different but largely similar ways made it into the very foundation of theology. Schleiermacher put more emphasis on the historically existent, the concrete particular within this perspective; Hegel had a clearer and firmer grasp of the overall structure of history because of his sure foundation in the concept of evolution, and he has therefore exercised the greater influence in the shaping of theology. The correlated ideas of the essence of religion, the development of this essence in the history of religion, and Christianity as the absolute religion, have arisen out of this background to become the apologetic foundation of the so-called modern or liberal theology. This theology, despite the different nuances it has added, presupposes this foundation at every point, and even the more supernaturally tinged systems have borrowed heavily from it. It is also the source of attempts to comprehend the history of Christianity in such a way as to show that critical historical research proves the person of Jesus to be the bearer of, and point of breakthrough for, the absolute religion. The absolute principle realized in and through him then serves as the idea or dynamic principle of Christianity, the further historical development of which is construed and evaluated on the basis of this one integral concept.[2]

It is against this background that the meaning of the problem posed in the present inquiry is to be understood.

The term "absoluteness" derives from the modern evolutionary apologetic and has a precise meaning only under its presuppositions. It has this precise meaning to the extent that it includes the horizons of the history of religion generally, the acknowledgment of all non-Christian religions as relative truths, and the interpretation of Christianity in relation to these relative truths as the absolute and completed form of religion. The term, its presuppositions, and its content are thus modern academic concepts through and through, conditioned by a leveling process in which all human events are drawn into the modern understanding of history.

Nevertheless, the evolutionary apologetic is closely related, in its motive and goal, to the apologetic of supernatural, orthodox theology. This point is to be stressed emphatically, and in this connection the following critical reflections, based on a nonspeculative understanding of history, should be mentioned. In its contemporary form the orthodox, supernatural apologetic does take the modern idea of history into account in that it subordinates external miracle to inner and in that the only essential function it attributes to inner miracle is that of assuring absolute certainty of salvation.[3] Those features of external miracle that are not absolutely necessary to the assertion and confirmation of the inner are sacrificed to the modern understanding of history. Both schools strive to establish the normative value of Christian thought. Indeed, endeavors of this kind are a matter of course for theology inasmuch as this discipline is in any reckoning the pursuit of normative religious knowledge and not merely an interest in the history of religion in general. Yet both the evolutionary and the orthodox schools of thought desire to attain this normative value by placing Christianity, as a matter of principle, in a unique position. They are not content with a *de facto* supremacy and ultimacy but want to make it into the sole truth to which everything else stands opposed in accordance with the requirements of theory. This attribution of a unique position to Christianity on the basis of a theoretical demand with a universal orientation is characteristic of both. What must emerge by necessity from universal, cosmic relationships as the content of divine truth is by nature, for both schools, not merely the highest and ultimate truth for man as he observes life about him, but the one and therefore the only truth about God and the world, about time and eternity. The two conceptions differ only in the means by which the implications of this idea are worked out.

The orthodox, supernatural apologetic secures a unique position for Christianity by reflections relating to the *form* in which religious truths arise. According to this way of thinking, man is made for full knowledge of God as shown by the very structure of creation which flows forth from the love of God and culminates in man. Cut off from the light of knowledge by the darkness of sin, man nevertheless retains a basic and intrinsic impulse toward God and the hope that someday there will be a manifestation of the fullness of divine truth. Since, however, everything human remains subjective, fallible, sinful, and powerless, what is required is a manifestation that will proceed from superhuman divine powers, a manifestation that will be recognized as divine precisely because it transcends and nullifies all likeness to human events. A manifestation is needed that will prove itself divine in its substantive effects by openly cleaving through the ordinary laws of the inner life of man. Miracle in the realm of nature, as attested in the accounts of the origin of Christianity, and the psychological miracle of conversion, which continues to the present day, guarantee this unique Christian causality. They confirm the reality of what all religious thought demands, namely, the manifestation of a religious truth and of a power for life that in principle lies beyond all human fallibility and impotence.

With this, however, the orthodox, supernatural apologetic is content. Its demand for "absoluteness" is satisfied when Christianity has been traced to an immediate divine causality, necessarily postulated by the religious man and present in his experience of this reality. It is satisfied when Christianity has been defined in principle as something that stands in opposition to everything human and historical, in opposition to all merely relative truths and powers. Absoluteness here consists of miracle. It is the absoluteness of a Christian Sunday causality in antithesis to the relativity and mediacy of a non-Christian weekday causality. The principle of supernaturalism is decisive. In relation to the religious content of the manifestation itself, on the other hand, this theology is deeply permeated by two ideas: first, that up to now we have received only a down payment and pledge of the truth; second, that anxiety, guilt, and sin have been overcome but that the divine light with its perfect clarity has sent only one of its rays into the midst of a vast, profound darkness. There is no mention of a religious knowledge that exhausts its underlying principle but only of a kind of religious knowledge that is set apart from everything else that poses as religion by features externally similar to those of the other religions. The decisive factor is a power attested in direct divine communication and therefore secure against admixture with all merely human wisdom. What matters is the power that draws the soul up into an otherwise inaccessible higher realm, even though this realm remains largely hidden from our eyes. For this reason the expression "absoluteness of Christianity" was not coined by holders of this view. They fashioned only the theory of exclusively supernatural revelation, in contrast to which everything outside Christianity stands as the work not of God but of man. What this apologetic understands by the term "absoluteness" is actually exclusive supernaturalism.[4]

The contrast with the evolutionary apologetic, however, lies precisely at this point. This apologetic has learned to abstain from impracticable attempts to secure for Christianity a favored position based on form. It seeks, therefore, by reference to *content and essence* to demonstrate that the idea of Christianity is to be recognized, in accordance with the requirements of theory, as the realization of the idea of religion itself. Here "human" and "divine" are not antithetical terms. Instead, everything is human and divine at the same time. Modern thought, it is held, has proved irrefutably the thoroughgoing continuity of the causal process and has made the dogmatic supernaturalism of the church impossible. It can, however, regard this causal context as a form for the realization of the "idea," here thought of as unfolding its inner life-content in gradual movement through the structures of causality. The idea, therefore, is regarded as containing within itself the movement of the divine life as a causal, teleological, and unitary life-process. Accordingly, this idea is present at every point in the universe, and it can be reconstructed from any given point. For finite consciousness, however, it becomes the consciously held idea of God or the idea of religion. This idea must first, therefore, gradually reveal its content and essence within the total meaning and context of human reality and in conjunction with man's unfolding of the depths of his own consciousness. But the idea must also attain the perfect goal, the absolute principle, in which all that was previously revealed as circumscribed, in process, and preliminary finds its ultimate conclusion.

All religion is, therefore, truth from God, each religion corresponding to some stage in a universal process of spiritual development. But there must also be a highest, ultimate stage that demonstrates itself to be so through its fulfillment of the evolutionary law intrinsic to the universal principle that is the basis of all things. What discloses the holy and abiding ground of all inner life to the faithful is not an apologetic of miracle and conversion but reflective meditation on the eternal content of Christian thought. The man of faith sees this inner principle evolving everywhere according to strict laws that follow from the nature of divine activity. On the basis of these laws of evolutionary development, he recognizes in devout admiration the inevitable preeminence of the summit on which he stands. From this summit he commands a view over all the divine powers of earthly history and reverently foresees the ultimate completion of all the purposes and powers at work in this history. From this perspective, tangled reality becomes crystal clear and what seemed to be chaos is transformed into a wondrous realm of transparently obvious consequences. A kind of religious geology teaches such a man to understand all lands and provinces in this realm as preliminary stages to the summit they all help to form, the summit that exists not in isolation from all else but simply as the crown of the whole. Of course this is not absolute knowledge of God—only God himself possesses that—but it is the absolute realization of all human knowledge of God, a realization that exhausts its principle and its substantive goal. This means it is *the* knowledge of God that man, as he proceeds from and returns to God, can understand as the finite spirit which, though rooted in infinity, consumes and purifies its finitude in devotion.

Only in this context does the expression "absoluteness" possess its full meaning. It signifies the perfect self-comprehension of the idea that strives for complete clarity, the self-realization of God in the human consciousness. It is the philosophical substitute for the dogmatic supernaturalism of the church.

Both the orthodox and the evolutionary theories thus take it for granted that the proof of normative religious truth can be provided only by the doctrine of a theoretically necessary and uniquely confirmed development of the religious powers of mankind. This is why these theories are so powerful and appealing. The problem of the normative, seen in relation to the multiplicity of history, appears most certainly resolved if the normative is something more than what we are able to recognize as normative by ourselves, if it is the sole and eternal truth, recognizable as such on the basis of a systematically worked-out concept. However embarrassed we feel in face of the centuries-old but increasingly inadequate, improbable, and confused artifices of the supernatural apologetic in areas of research relating to the Bible and church history, we nevertheless find ourselves strongly attracted time and again by its religious thought. Yet most people are only alienated by a path to knowledge that, when concretely applied, cannot avoid defects of this kind.

Where alienation from this path occurs, however, the only alternative that appears to remain is that of the evolutionary apologetic. It too continually attracts religious persons by the depth and breadth of its perspective, by the mighty power of its all-embracing vision, by the pure energy that consumes all husks and forms in the flame of thought. It too allures religious people by its staunch faith in the meaning and coherence of the divine activity in the world, its faith which, cutting through all distractions and confusions, unerringly points like a compass to the one, eternal, divine idea. However difficult it may be for this apologetic to transform the totality of earthly affairs into a translucent crystal through which the powers of the idea may radiate with formative effect, nevertheless, if the other approach has been closed, and if a way is expected to exist, then this appears to be the only way. If the isolation of Christianity from other historical phenomena as an absolute, uniquely grounded truth and the tracing of this uniqueness to a special Christian causality is no longer a live alternative, then it is all the more certain that the goal must be reached by means of the concept of that which is common to all religions and by the realization of this exclusively true and universal principle in Christianity.

These two theories, therefore, are the only ones that require serious consideration in an inquiry concerning the "absoluteness" of Christianity. They alone have a clear-cut and worthy concept behind them and have seriously undertaken to support and explicate this concept. The popular disdain in which many theologians today hold these theories is superficial and thoughtless. These theories take their revenge, though, in that they continually lend themselves to these theologians in piecemeal and inconsistent forms. Orthodoxy and Hegelian speculation have often been pronounced dead with profound feelings of superiority, but just as often their funeral orators have themselves made use of the forms that had been declared defunct, though in their use the foundation and inner spirit are lost.

Thus for many people today the expression "absoluteness of Christianity" has become a colorless concept that is treated with great passion indeed but with little concrete meaning. For many it is merely a modern, neutral-sounding, scholarly expression by which they really mean supernatural revelation, but they have no clear conceptual basis for this revelation; it is merely one of the many ill-fitting academic masks that are worn to the feast of theology. To others it signifies Christianity's character as the final and perfect religion. However, they are not even mildly disquieted by this perfection, even though the concepts that support it, including the concept of faith in an "idea" as a faith that consumes all empirical phenomena, continually call for further elucidation. To still others the term "absoluteness of Christianity" simply represents the claim Christianity makes to exclusive truth, a claim which, though it conflicts sharply with all similar claims, nevertheless belongs to the very nature of Christianity and therefore must simply be accepted. They do not take this to mean that the interpretation of Christian thought should exclude a flexible consideration of other kinds of truths and other ways of understanding, such as those of the natural sciences. Unfortunately, however, this theology that makes so much of the Christian claim takes no account of the corresponding claims of other religions.

Over against such facile, pallid ways of treating these extremely difficult and weighty concepts, which are particularly likely to baffle the beginning student of contemporary theology, what is really important is to grasp the problem in its own clear and definite meaning. Simple *normative value* is something distinct from exclusively *supernatural revelation* and likewise from *absolute fulfillment of the principle of religion*. The latter two, again, are essentially different from one another and cannot be united.

With regard to the antithesis between these latter two, no one should be deceived by hybrid forms of long standing that modern mediating theology frequently appeals to and praises as blending both types of apologetic. When early Christianity first entered into the educated world, it had to commit itself decisively to an encounter with other religions. It established its relationship to them—to Judaism, to the doctrines and cults that were then advancing from Asia, to the old national religions, and to the philosophical religions of reform—in serious practical struggles and intellectual labor. Of course it was not the approach of the comparative history of religions with its preponderantly theoretical problems but the environment of mutually hostile religions and the consequent necessity of making both practical and theoretical decisions that provided the context within which early Christian theology took shape. Here the apostle Paul, the first to perceive the Christian faith as a new, independent, and universal religious power, was the forerunner. His treatment of the problem, however, relied disproportionately on Judaism, simply presupposing the Jewish and Hellenized-Jewish apologetic against the heathen. On the other hand, it depended too much on inner and unrepeatable personal experiences—the appearance of Christ, his inner struggle with the Law, and his possession by the Spirit—to be intelligible or satisfying to later generations.

The problem was taken up as a matter of principle for the first time when Christianity encountered Gnosticism. It was in the debate with Gnosticism, while partly rejecting and partly utilizing it, that institutional Christianity adopted its definitive position. In this contest it forged its first and strongest coat of armor: the doctrines of supernatural divine revelation and incarnation. It used these doctrines to argue that Christian faith meant perfect and final knowledge of God, that it was something essentially new and "absolute." But over this suit of armor, forged by the uncultured faith of the congregation, it learned to wear yet another, which was fashioned by the philosophers of the church. This was the theory that all moments of truth as contained in other cults, mythologies, philosophical systems, and moral teachings are expressions of the divine Reason that is at work in the natural world, and that these instances of truth are comprehended in enhanced, purified, and therefore perfect form, in Christ, the incarnation of the divine Reason. Christianity is thus both the revelation of previously concealed divine mysteries and the truth of natural reason in "absolute" form.

This proof of "absoluteness" has its center, first and foremost, in the theory of supernatural revelation. The subsequently added doctrine of the identity of the God revealed in Christ with the universal divine Reason and with the natural moral law actually belongs to a mode of thought that is peculiar to antiquity. This mode of thought is poles away from the idea of a historical development of religion culminating in the Christian knowledge of God in any sense that would combine sober historical criticism with a teleological view of history. In particular it is far removed from considering the history of *religion* as *history* of religion. On the contrary, the breakdown of national religions and cultural values, and the conflicts that then occurred, resulted, for the period of antiquity, in a completely unhistorical generalization of certain metaphysical and ethical concepts and an utterly fantastic syncretism that arbitrarily combined with these concepts the images and myths of the disintegrated and uprooted national religions.[5] All attempts at religious reform seized on this rationalistic and syncretistic mode of thought, and the religion it served with the greatest success of all was Christianity. To Christianity the non-Christian religions were by no means religions in the true sense of the word, and it was utterly devoid of any concept of religion as a species. Christianity itself was revelation and not religion. Other religions were sporadic and distorted philosophical systems based on a natural knowledge of God. But in the clarity of the divine light these systems were fully comprehended, it was believed, in Christianity, though here they were set free of their otherwise natural instability because of the foundation provided by the miracle of revelation.

For the declining culture, this blend of ideas constituted a spiritual rescue, and in terms of the intellectual climate of late antiquity, it was thoroughly justified. But this view has little in common with the thought behind the evolutionary apologetic, and even as employed by the supernatural apologetic, it has increasingly tended to become a mere auxiliary idea. The old rationalistic and syncretistic view of religion, as far as the supernatural apologetic is concerned, has sunk to the level of a mere exemplification of religious drives and needs that are found in men universally and that play a part in every religion. It has sunk to the level of a set of questions that find their answer only in the Christian revelation, people forgetting that these questions and needs are themselves products of Christianity and of its most closely related precursors.

Consequently, this entire sketch of how the relationship between Christianity and other religions was conceived in the early church has very little connection with the modern, historically conceived problem as to the "absoluteness" of Christianity in relation to other religions. This problem remains focused exclusively on the two great theories, one relying on the absolute miracle of an inner renewal that transcends all natural powers, and the other finding its support in the realization of the essence of religion in Christianity, defending this concept by reference to the history of evolution.

The first of these theories, however, can never prove its validity merely by appealing to purely internal experience or its content. On this basis it can arrive only at the recognition that over and above that dimension of human life which is bound by natural conditions there is also a higher life of the human spirit. As for the different forms of this higher life that emerge in the various religions and in other creations of the human spirit, this theory can distinguish between them only as to their depth and power. But when it tries to prove on this basis that Christianity occupies a unique position, it constantly finds itself obliged to argue for a specifically Christian miraculous causality that breaks through natural causality in this inner experience. This line of thought requires it to find external substantiation for its purely internal miraculous causality, and it does so by reference to the archetypal miracles of the incarnation and of the time of the founding of Christianity. Inner miracles that defy the homogeneity of history are not as such capable of demonstration. Their uniquely miraculous character demands support from the great, external, archetypal miracles. But with this, the theory as a whole is forced into that well-known apologetic which must differentiate sacred from profane events and which, along with its arguments for this dichotomy, gasps for breath the more it breathes the air of the modern understanding of history.

We are left, therefore, with the idealistic-evolutionary theory as the only one that calls for serious critical consideration. In itself this theory is an attempt to rule out every means of isolating Christianity from the rest of history on the basis of miracle, and it is an attempt to present in a purely historical way the validity and significance of the Christian religion in statements as unequivocal as the doctrinal formulations of the early church. The entire flowering of theology during the first part of the nineteenth century was due to this theory. It stimulated research in the areas of Bible, church history, and history of Christian doctrine, and provided a basis for overcoming the tension between faith and history. To this day it offers itself wherever men find the church's idea of history untenable, and for many who are not in contact with the more exact development of doctrine, its propositions constitute a message of liberation even today.[6]

The problem is, therefore, whether this theory of the absoluteness of Christianity as the realization of the idea of religion is a tenable alternative to the doctrine of exclusive supernatural revelation. This includes the problem of whether the idealistic and evolutionary theory of absoluteness can, for its part, answer the momentous and radical question of our intellectual, or at least of our religious, situation. This question is: How can we pass beyond the diversity with which history presents us to norms for our faith and for our judgments about life?

The reflections set forth in the following section will be devoted to this problem. The outcome of these reflections is essentially negative, but the reflections themselves do not call into question the general presupposition upon which this theory depends, namely, its underlying conception of history. The purpose of these reflections is, rather, on the basis of this conception of history, to find a solution to the problem that will be less vulnerable to serious objections.

2
REEXAMINATION
OF THE
EVOLUTIONARY
APOLOGETIC

It is impossible to construct a theory of Christianity as the absolute religion on the basis of a historical way of thinking or by the use of historical means. Much that looks weak, shadowy, and unstable in the theology of our day is rooted in the impossibility of putting such a construction on Christianity.

Thus our conclusion may be indicated from the very outset, for historians have sought for a hundred years, with increasingly refined and autonomous methods, to make this construction practicable. A true understanding of history presupposes universal structures of law only in the form of physical and anthropological conditions, on the one hand, and in the form of basic psychological drives and sociological laws, on the other. Its primary focus of interest lies, however, in what takes shape out of these conditions and within this network and for that reason alone is capable of being depicted historically. Its chief concern is with the unique and individual.

Uniqueness and individuality, however, while characteristic of everything historical, stem, for their part, from an inner movement of life that cannot be reduced to a prior cause, and they also have their source in the correlative interconnection of all historical events. Given this interrelation, the factors that come together under specific conditions to produce a given result, even if it be one of the most general or far-reaching significance, present this result as something possible only at this one particular place. They present it as something that is at bottom a uniquely conditioned disclosure of life, especially of that creative life which comes to expression in the intellectual, cultural, and religious dimensions of human existence. Yet as far as this creative life is concerned, it is impossible, at least *a posteriori,* to strip away the particularity of a given phenomenon and then distill from the remainder a concealed but operative universal. The impossibility of proceeding in this way is shown by the fact that the idea of a universal, wherever it arises, is itself brought into being in terms of particular historical conditions. It can arise only by effecting what becomes a historically necessary departure from the living content that dominated whatever form preceded it, and it always takes shape in relation to definite intellectual and ethical influences of a given situation and moment.

Furthermore, our theories as to general laws of evolution and as to the values found in history are themselves historically and individually conditioned in every case by the standpoint from which they are formulated. More particularly, from the angle of vision afforded by the modern understanding of history there always exists an indissoluble distinction between the perceptions, thoughts, and desires that accompany man as a physical entity in the realm of nature and the higher, creative element in man that intervenes and opposes them. This higher, creative element, for all its involvement in perceptions, thoughts, and desires of this kind, leads its own autonomous life and can therefore under no circumstances be classified with them under the concept of a single, all-embracing causal principle. The modern understanding of history sees an encounter between opposed forces wherever it looks, and it has only muddied the waters of historical understanding when it has incorporated monistic theories into its work. The modern idea of history, as it has taken shape in connection with the object of its inquiries, knows no concept of a universal principle that embodies a law governing the successive generation of individual historical realities. It knows no basis which would allow all phenomena to be grasped immanently by means of an all-inclusive principle that would constitute, first, a law regulating the emergence and evolution of everything individual; second, and for this very reason, the essence and fulfillment of all genuine value; and third, the norm of all historical phenomena. For that which comes into being within history in relation to norms, values, and ideals that possess universal *validity*, there must be a foundation other than that implied in their reduction to the common denominator of *existence*. This foundation, though not easily knowable in the profusion of individual forms it produces, should be accessible to analysis that seeks to abstract what is invariable from changing individual phenomena.

These fundamental principles are at work in all important historical studies. Among the many accounts of the history of Christianity, it is those guided consciously or instinctively by these principles which strike us as most vibrant and penetrating. Wellhausen's *Geschichte Israels* [History of Israel], Jülicher's *Die Einleitung in das Neue Testament* [Introduction to the New Testament] and his *Die Gleichnisreden Jesu* [The Parables of Jesus], and Harnack's *Dogmengeschichte* [History of Dogma] make a strong impact precisely for this reason. If this point is borne in mind, it is easy to spot the error behind attempts to interpret Christianity as the absolute religion, for it gives us a certain sense of disquiet much the same as that we feel when we turn from historical books of this quality to doctrinaire historical introductions in works of systematic theology.

Introductions of this kind attempt to survey the total phenomenon of the religious life of mankind or of the so-called "essence of religion." These surveys comprise, as is natural, the opening section of such theological works, but it is by no means merely because of the defectiveness of our knowledge that they have proved unfeasible. According to the usual procedure, it is essential in such surveys to draw out by psychological methods what is common to, or typical of, all religious phenomena and to attach to this typical result the broader epistemological and ontological questions as to the reality of the object affirmed in religion. But these surveys do not stop with this important and necessary treatment of the concept of what is universal in religion. To this concept is added that of a universal "essence" which provides above all the idea of a norm. This norm does more than make it possible to appraise individual religions according to their value, for in the religions the norm reaches definitive and exhaustive realization. Thus this universal principle or essence of religion is regarded as a power that brings forth all the individual religions according to an immanent law. It is a power that produces in these individual phenomena not only special instances of the universal law but, more important, a teleological series of successive self-realizations of the universal principle, culminating in its complete and exhaustive manifestation. Christianity is viewed as the termination of the series and hence as the absolute realization of the principle. This applies, however, not to its concrete historical forms but to its "essence" as established by abstraction.

This "essence of Christianity," moreover, is thought of as related to the concrete individual forms of the Christian religion in the same way that the essence of religion is related to the concrete religions. Just as these religions must be understood on the basis of the universal principle that is immanent within them, so Christianity must be understood on the basis of the universal principle that is realized in it. As a general rule, a rather penetrating criticism of the Christian religion as an empirical phenomenon accompanies these surveys.

The basic ideas of this interpretation are clear. First, it subordinates history to the concept of a universal principle which represents a uniform, homogeneous, law-structured, and self-actuating power that brings forth individual instances of itself. Second, it elevates this concept of a universal principle to that of a norm and ideal representing what is of permanent value in all events. Third, it binds these two concepts together by means of a theory of evolutionary development. This implies, as the fourth basic idea, both a perfect congruity between the results of the law-regulated causal process as brought forth in accordance with the concept of the universal principle and the successive creation of value as produced in accordance with the concept of absolute realization.

The irrefutable objections to this interpretation are, however, equally clear. The modern idea of history knows no universal principle on the basis of which the content and sequence of events might be deduced. It knows only concrete, individual phenomena, always conditioned by their context and yet, at bottom, underivable and simply existent phenomena. For this reason the modern understanding of history knows no values or norms that coincide with actual universals. It knows them, rather, strictly as universally valid ideas, or ideas purporting to be universally valid, which invariably appear in individual form and make their universal validity known by their resistance to the merely existent. For all these reasons the modern understanding of history knows no evolutionary development in which an actual, law-regulated universal principle produces values that are universally authentic. It knows, finally, no absolute realization of such a universal principle within the context of history where, as a matter of fact, only phenomena that are uniquely defined and limited and thus possess individual character are brought forth at any given point.

The defects in the basic ideas of this interpretation appear even more clearly in their results. This holds true for each of the four main points.

First, our knowledge of the history of religions is indeed incomplete, but at least with regard to the principal phenomena it is now so firmly established that it is no longer possible to formulate the concept of a universal principle or essence of religion in such a way as to make it include both a normative principle and the necessity for a graduated manifestation of this realized normative principle. Of course it may be claimed that the universal principle here under consideration is not conceived as a law under which individual cases are to be subsumed but as a principle that unites causality and finality, a principle that contains in every moment of its operation an intimation of the goal toward which it strives. Yet even where this view is adhered to, it still remains impossible to see in the lower stages the higher stages toward which they lead, or to see in the higher a continuation of the lower. Instead, this approach invariably leads to concepts and definitions of the essence of religion that do not yet fit the lower stages and no longer fit the higher. It leads to vague notions which must then be inserted by the power of imagination into discrete empirical phenomena as their germinative nucleus. Or it leads to setting up concepts of religion which are for the most part merely watered-down versions of Christianity (and these, as is easily understood, are especially beloved by the theologians), whereupon Christianity is simply designated, without any seriously reasoned basis, as the ideal religion toward which all things tend. Or again, this approach leads to crediting the concrete religions with something that is actually a form of religious apprehension inspired by metaphysical reflections, this generally being the case with pantheizing concepts of religion influenced by the modern understanding of nature.

In all these cases it becomes evident that the concepts men sought to weld together in a theory of this kind have now come apart. The concept of that which is really and authentically universal in the basic and characteristic phenomena of religion and the concept of a norm governing authoritative religious truth were appended to each distinctive, historical religion seen as a concrete, individual phenomenon. These concepts, precisely because their definitions are so obscure and uncertain, show clearly how impossible it is to take a universal principle or essence and suddenly give it normative status or, conversely, to defend the concept of a normative principle by reference to its concurrent property of being a universal one.

Even more serious, in the second place, is what happens with regard to the absolute realization of this universal principle in the process of historical development. Here two possibilities exist. On the one hand, greater emphasis may be laid on the causal aspect of the universal principle. In this case, however, its absolute realization is embodied only in the sequence of historical configurations taken as a whole. Among these configurations, then, there can obviously be no absolute religion in which this principle or essence is exclusively and exhaustively realized. "The idea prefers not to pour out all its abundance into one individual specimen." However plausible such a view may appear to the historian, since it enables him to form conceptions freely and impartially, it can hardly suffice for him who sees in religion not merely an object of historical inquiry but a question of life itself and who for this reason is even less inclined to forget the teleological aspect of the universal principle. Yet at the same time it is the historian himself who cannot evade the teleological problem, inasmuch as he pursues his labors not merely for the sake of gaining knowledge of things past but rather for the sake of comprehending the values that gradually make themselves known in history.

If the aspect of gradual manifestation is given the stronger emphasis, however, then the second possibility comes into view. One senses that he is indeed oriented toward a goal, but he feels that until the end of history is reached, he ought not to speak of an absolute religion but should await it in close conjunction with the end of all history. There must be complete twilight before the owl of Minerva can begin its flight in the land of the realized absolute principle. But if that is how matters stand, how can the universal principle be characterized with sufficient certainty as long as its definitive realization still lies far off in the incalculable distance? And if the character of the universal principle cannot be determined with certainty, how then can its stages be described with certainty—those stages by which it has moved toward realization up to the present time and among which we are supposed to make a choice? Precisely for this reason, the attempt to demonstrate a religion as absolute never continues long with one historical religion but tends to become a projection of the religion of the future. The impracticability of this concept of absolute realization is made unmistakably evident, however, by the fact that these depictions of the coming religion, each of which is set forth as the goal of the evolutionary process, are mutually inconsistent. As a result, there is great disparity in the determination and evaluation of the stages that lead to this goal, the highest being the one on which we are supposed to take our stand.

More specifically, the modern study of history gives no indication whatever of any graded progression such as this theory might lead us to expect. History manifests no gradual ascent to higher orientations as far as the vast majority of mankind is concerned. Only at special points do higher orientations burst forth, and then in a great, soaring development of their uniquely individual content. By no means, however, are the great religions that burst forth in this way related to each other in a stage-by-stage causal process. They stand, rather, in a parallel relationship. The only path to an understanding of their relationship in terms of value is toil and inner moral struggle, not schemes of progressive development like those that are always being constructed. Since it is no longer merely the history of religion in the Near East and in the cultures around the Mediterranean but also the world of the East Asian religions that stands before our eyes, we can no longer deceive ourselves about this matter. Thus even with regard to this aspect, our conclusion is that while the modern study of history cannot avoid forming concepts of normative principles, it cannot arrive at such concepts by proofs for the absolute realization of a universal principle.

Most problematic of all, in the third place, is the interpreting of Christianity as the absolute religion. This holds true not only because, as suggested above, no such demonstration is possible in historical terms, but above all because the impossibility of uniting a theoretically conceived universal principle with a concrete, individual, historical configuration becomes directly discernible at this point. Of course all religious men naturally understand that Christianity is a dynamic religious orientation of great significance, that it is under all circumstances an eminent religious truth. Yet it is also evident that Christianity in every age, and particularly in its period of origin, is a genuinely historical phenomenon —new, by and large, in its consequences, but profoundly and radically conditioned by the historical situation and environment in which it found itself as well as by the relations it entered into in its further development. It presupposes the breakdown of the ethnic religions of antiquity and also of the naïve values that had sprung up with them. It likewise presupposes the new religious movements that emerged from this rubble and then gravitated toward Christianity as the most powerful force. Indeed, these movements may possibly have participated in some way in Christianity's earliest, formative history.

In its central concepts, moreover, Christianity is clearly determined in a radical sense by the eschatological ideas that were a source of strength to Israel in this situation. It was in connection with these ideas that Christianity first articulated its purely inward and ethical faith. At this particular juncture, however, the early Christian ethic was so strongly stamped by the expectation of the end of the world and of standing in the presence of God, as well as by indifference to all earthly values, that it took on the religious harshness and one-sidedness that is possible only in such situations and under such presuppositions. Yet no sooner had Christianity freed itself from these first popular and mythical forms and disclosed its concern for humane and inward values than it drew to itself the closely related ethics of Platonism and Stoicism together with the metaphysics of idealism and the teleology of Aristotelianism. Thus it showed again, by virtue of these relations, that it was a thoroughly concrete, limited, and conditioned movement.

And so it continues to the present day. Nowhere is Christianity the absolute religion, an utterly unique species free of the historical conditions that comprise its environment at any given time. Nowhere is it the changeless, exhaustive, and unconditioned realization of that which is conceived as the universal principle of religion.

To be sure, it is necessary to seek out the controlling idea of Christianity and to understand, as far as possible, the development and continuation of Christianity in view of the content of this idea. But this controlling idea must be derived strictly from Christianity, which means that it is at every moment intimately interwoven with quite definite historical conditions. Like all other ideas, it lives by virtue of its involvement in a historical context and thus always in completely individual, historical forms. Conversely, this controlling idea is falsified and placed in an utterly artificial relationship to its own reality if it is contrived from without as the absolute idea of religion and then injected into Christianity.

This is the point, therefore, where the difficulties and artifices of theology stand out most prominently. Kernel and husk, form and content, abiding truth and temporal-historical conditions— these are the formulas of which amazing use is frequently made to help theology escape from this labyrinth. Yet the result of these various attempts is that the actual absoluteness of the kernel always absolutizes the husk as well, while the actual relativity of the husk always relativizes the kernel in turn. "The temporal-historical form for the realization of the absolute ideal" reminds one, more than anything else, of molten iron in a wax container or of solid paraffin in a red-hot mold. Such a distinction is possible only as regards peripheral minutiae. Where matters of substance are concerned, the most important religious ideas are the ones that are most closely bound up with the leading ideas of a given period, even though these leading ideas may be utterly alien to us and impossible for us to reproduce in our experience today.

Thus the outcome of all this busy drawing of distinctions is simply that it becomes increasingly difficult to see what difference they make, and any mounting joy in the magnificent individual reality of history is lost. What was once lightly set aside as husk is now receiving proper recognition in authentic historical studies, not because it is of primary importance but because what is primarily important is not an ahistorical, eternal, and ever unfolding principle but a living, individual complex of concrete reality, a whole that has become what it is under very specific conditions. In this whole the precipitate of innumerable historical developments is carried forward, always controlled and shaped by its own inner necessity, yet also capable of bestowing substance and justification on the needs of each new period in all their ramifications. All this simply shows us, however, that it is historical reality itself which shatters every attempt to interpret Christianity on the basis of the concept of an absolute, self-fulfilling principle. Whatever the significance of Christianity may be, neither its origin nor its history nor again its importance in the history of religions will ever be known from its alleged identity with the absolute principle of religion.

Similar objections ensue, finally, in the case of the comprehensive concept that dominates all these different consequences of the theory of absolute realization—the concept of evolutionary development itself. In and of itself this concept is one of the most reliable working tools there is, and it is one of the fundamental presuppositions of the scientific study of history. It has proved its worth beyond all shadow of doubt and corresponds to all knowable processes in the sense that everywhere, whether in large matters or small, elemental points of departure have to be assumed, on the basis of which the more complex life of matter and spirit arises through a combination of resistance and assimilation. It is equally certain that all the great creative urges, ideas, and animating powers that break forth in this evolutionary process first appeared in primitive, embryonic forms and disclosed their true content only in accommodation and antithesis, in growing depth and unfolding of implications, in reflection and struggle that lasted through many generations. To an outlook that faces the past, the forces that have burst forth in this way must accordingly appear as life-principles or creative energies that develop in accordance with their own inner logic.

At this point, however, everything hinges on the way of thinking or conception as to the nature of evolutionary development in human affairs, on the one hand, and in concrete, individual events, on the other.

Speculative evolutionism is characterized by its conception of the total life of mankind as an evolutionary sequence in which a creative, teleological force generates the entire causal dynamic for the subsequent inwardly motivated acts that follow one upon the other in a definite order logically requisite to attaining their goal. Out of this congruity of finality and causality, speculative evolutionism abstracts laws that permit it not only to judge the level of each separate phenomenon in accordance with a personal ethical appraisal as to how close it is to its goal, but also to do all this on the basis of ordered sequences in a causally conceived evolutionary process and thus in accordance with the demands of theory. Speculative evolutionism has its sole support in an evolutionary metaphysic of the absolute, a metaphysic which, as mentioned above, brings about a convergence of causality and finality in the concept of the absolute and is open to serious ethical and religious objections. But quite apart from such considerations, this speculative construction, when viewed from the perspective of the modern idea of history, stands in utter contradiction to real events.

Seen in terms of the modern understanding of history, a rigorously consistent causal structure, capable of being formulated in universal laws, can be demonstrated historically only by reference to needs and perceptions that are bound to the natural foundations of existence. But when it comes to the bursting forth of the higher, creative powers in human life, powers that exist as dynamic principles necessary in themselves and that stand over against the kinds of motivations that derive from nature, the modern idea of history can neither recognize the force behind such eruptions as the force that underlies all causal processes and brings them to fulfillment, nor can it explain this force as a phenomenon that necessarily follows from its basis in nature. It can only point to favorable or unfavorable alignments of natural psychological processes, alignments that either facilitate and promote, or hinder and distort, the emergence of the higher, creative forces in human life. It can regard them only as independent powers that are directed toward the will and possess their own inner logic, powers whose origin and action it must study with the same impartial dedication that it does the operation of motivations most closely associated with natural needs.

The modern idea of history recognizes, therefore, a struggle between two radically different influences in human life, influences that are indeed interrelated but neither of which can be explained by the other. Human life, in this view, is by no means thought of as a series of events that can be reduced to a causally understood sequence of essentially homogeneous acts. It is thought of, rather, as possessing a mysterious double nature. In this nature the difficult concepts of freedom and personality are of fundamental significance, since motivation which springs from the higher, creative powers is never a mere extension of previously activated natural motivations, and since the emergence of such powers takes place not as the result of a simple adding up of antecedent effects but as a result of original developments that arise from a deeper foundation. In practice, therefore, every theoretical account of the stages of the evolutionary process which is merely systematic and dialectical represents a doctrinaire assault on real history. Only in the obscure area of prehistory has research of this kind been left with a field to cultivate, and in the tendentious tracing of all cultural developments to economic causes, its caricature lives on today.

Genuinely significant history-writing, however, has freed itself from this kind of research. It regularly presents its ideas of evolutionary development as nothing more than pictures of the interrelation of cultural structures. It makes these pictures as true to life as possible, but it does not permit its explanations or its evaluations to be bound to doctrinaire preconceptions. Doctrinaire interpretation is thwarted not only by the concreteness and individuality found in history taken purely as such but, more particularly, by the foundation that the most important and definitive historical configurations have in independent higher powers which cannot themselves be incorporated into a theoretically postulated sequence. That is why, in the history of religions today, deductions regarding the history of evolution are limited to the so-called "beginnings" and to the uncivilized forms of religion, where the lack of reliable sources and the difficulty of ascertaining people's religious sentiments allow this theory freer play. When it comes to the great world religions, however, contemporary historians present them as unique movements shaped and defined by their own situations and presuppositions, movements whose nature and content cannot be known except by direct study of these religions. Even students of the history of Christianity have more and more clearly moved away from misleading scale-oriented theories in which primitive Christianity, Catholicism, and Protestantism are treated as logically related members of an ascending series. No period is a mere rung on a ladder; each one possesses, in context, its own nature and self-sufficient meaning. It is this realization that underlies the remarkable advances made by recent studies in church history as over against the schematic approach of the Tübingen school.

Thus in this case too our conclusion may be expressed as follows: Whatever the permanent significance of the concept of evolutionary development may be, it is not to be worked out in the form of a sequence that assumes a congruity between causality and finality and thus seems to make possible a theoretical computation of the value of the various stages. It is not to be used to prove the absoluteness of any one religion as the definitive realization of the principle of religion itself.[1]

It is evident, therefore, that the attempt to present Christianity as the absolute religion is untenable. The fathers of the theology of evolutionary development found it possible to put a construction like this on Christianity only because the history of religion of their day was still quite undeveloped and provincial. Equally important, their historical research into the Christian religion still fluctuated between rationalistic-pragmatic explanations of individual phenomena, on the one hand, and poetic-intuitive improvisations, on the other. Only through the mist of historical knowledge that was still quite hazy could the rainbow of such speculation shine.

Moreover, these theologians still stood under the influence of an older habit of thought that saw Christianity as the divine realization of natural religion, of the Logos, and of the natural moral law. Their "essence of religion," seen from that angle, was simply a flexible version of natural religion. Their "realization of the principle of religion in Christianity" was simply the poetic idea of natural religion made perfect and introduced into history by God. Thus old habits of thought still have power even over those who have broken away from them at critical points. Furthermore, in their use of this construction, these men were obliged to attach significant qualifications to it.

Schleiermacher, after declaring in his *Über die Religion: Reden an die gebildeten unter ihren Verächtern* [On Religion: Addresses in Response to Its Cultured Critics] that he would bar no book from becoming a Bible, later—in his theological and ecclesiastical period—developed an interpretation of Christianity as the realization of that essence of religion which is latent in creation and which evolves by means of the elevation of the spirit over the flesh. Yet at the same time he was careful to consider Christianity in its constantly individual and historically limited, hence always changeable, forms. It was he who coined the catchword "individual" (*das Individuelle*) and made it fruitful for a nondogmatic understanding of Christian history. For this reason it was also he who limited the absolute religion to a *single* point, to the person of Jesus, whom he then interpreted, in a sense that was actually both historical and dogmatic, as an archetypal redemptive figure of absolute, unconditioned, and unlimited religious knowledge and power, subject to change in appearance but in reality changeless. The effects proceeding from this original figure, however, he at once subsumed again under the category of history, holding that they were always to be understood not only as imperfect because of sin but also as necessarily limited because of their individual character.

Hegel, on the other hand, defined Christianity in its entirety as the absolute religion, for he perceived in it the highest and final stage of religion. In fact, however, it was for him merely the last of the preparatory stages that, though remaining limited to symbols, would lead to the absolute religion. This absolute religion was to evolve out of Christianity as a purely mental construct, but its truth could be demonstrated only by drawing inferences from the absolute principle inhering in the absolute idea that works itself out in history. Accordingly, the idea of the absolute religion was taken not from history but from the concept of the absolute itself. The concept of the absolute was regarded as a rationally necessary concept. It derived from and was utterly dependent on a rationally necessary concept of God, but it appeared in history only as an end product of thought. However, the connection between this concept and historical Christianity—most important, its connection with the person of Jesus taken as exhibiting this concept perfectly in a practical sense—is merely asserted, not demonstrated.

Thus both of these creative thinkers made only cautious, qualified use of the idea of Christianity as the absolute religion. Some of their theological heirs have handled this idea rather clumsily, but even their keenest students have either changed it back into the old, supernatural theory, or understood it as signifying the exclusion of every absolute from history. The numerous apostates and disappointed admirers of theology, who in that hopeful springtime of the renewal of theology left the Schleiermacherian and Hegelian schools, have made this state of affairs abundantly clear. Beginning with Bruno Bauer, whose work is unsystematic but instructive, and Renan, whose work lacks theoretical foundation but shows a fine feeling for history, these consequences have been brought out in their most general form by two prominent scholars—Strauss and Lagarde.

Strauss, who though admittedly not a profoundly religious man was a solid and perceptive scholar, has shown clearly and irrefutably—in opposition to Hegel—that no absolutely perfect principle of religion can be realized in history at any single point. He further demonstrated that the history of primitive Christianity, when scrutinized by rigorous historical methods, in no way proves to be that kind of a realization. He next went on to show just as incontrovertibly—in opposition to Schleiermacher—that it is impossible to postulate an absolute and historically unconditioned cause for individual and conditioned historical effects. He also showed that the picture of the person of Jesus as absolute, sketched on the basis of this postulate and confirmed by the sources through the use of an allegedly pure historical method, is an anemic abstraction full of internal contradictions. History is no place for "absolute religions" or "absolute personalities." Such terms are self-contradictory.

Lagarde, on the other hand, who possessed an earnest religious nature but was neither a keen dialectician nor a systematic thinker, divorced the evolutionary development of religion from all dogmatic and metaphysical applications and called for impartial, dedicated study of the history of religion that would make use of every available means for conscientious research. Study of this kind, in contrast to the chaotic tangles that philosophy and theology lead to, should permit one, he held, to acquire an understanding of the characteristic phenomena of religion, and on this foundation it should be possible to work out a purely historical assessment of Christianity. An assessment of this kind would in effect constitute, he believed, an overwhelming demonstration of the greatness and majesty of the Christianity that would emerge when freed of apologetic trimmings and ballast. At the same time, Lagarde went on, nothing certain could be said about subsequent developments in the history of religion, and the emergence of great new religious movements might even be imminent.

On the whole, it is criticism of this kind—and not the positive views of either man—that has won the day. Or to put it with greater precision, increasingly exact historical research has of itself discarded all such erroneous and misleading attempts to demonstrate Christianity as absolute. Increasingly refined historical inquiry has led to a more vital apprehension of the historically conditioned uniqueness of Christianity and to a more and more radical interweaving of the Christian religion into human history generally.

Works as mature and guarded as Weizsäcker's *Apostolisches Zeitalter* [The Apostolic Age] and Jülicher's *Die Gleichnisreden Jesu* [The Parables of Jesus], both of which have earned an impressive reputation everywhere, demonstrate this point more clearly than any abstract inquiry. Free of dogmatic and anti-dogmatic preconceptions, these works bring us face to face with historical reality. They speak, as historical knowledge must, with lacunae and uncertainties as well as reservations that look toward improved insights in the future, but also with clarity as to matters of fundamental importance. In this reality we find much that is high and noble, but nothing that might lead us to perceive the realized principle of religion as a kind of underlying motif. Everything of this kind is completely ruled out in the most recent development, which has brought research into the origins of Christianity under the influence of classical and Semitic philologists. What has been worked out in this connection, particularly by Usener and his school, is a purely philological method of inquiry based on the history of religion in the period of late antiquity. This approach raises for us a host of problems once thought of as settled. At times inquiries of this kind reveal something of the aversion that humanists and cultured aristocrats feel toward Christianity; yet they also set forth a convergence of historical currents in which Christianity stands forth not as a mere principle but as a highly complex configuration bearing the stamp of a definite period of history.

The consequences of all this labor—abandonment of the false

identification of the concept of universality with that of normativeness; renunciation of proofs for Christianity as the absolute
religion by means of a speculative philosophy of history; and
recognition of the limited, individual, and highly conditioned
character of all historical phenomena—have thus been acknowledged by large numbers of contemporary theologians.

One might think that a state of clarity had been attained,
were it not that the most recent and outstanding school of theology has made use of this acknowledgment in a most confused
way—in effect abrogating its consequences. True, the head of
this school, Albrecht Ritschl, has not himself incurred this reproach. He argues for the normativeness of Christianity on the
basis of a very simple combination of ethical postulates drawn
from the history of religion and supernatural authority. In terms
of this combination, Christianity is the miraculous realization of
the postulate that appears ever more clearly in the history of
religion—the postulate of the self-affirmation of moral personality
over the world.

Ritschl left the concept of miracle, which is so decisive for
such a view, in an odd state of suspense, preferring instead to
emphasize, on the one hand, Jesus' claim to be the absolute revelation of truth and, on the other, the devout self-certainty of the
Christian communion. Many of his followers, however, have
sought to define this matter more precisely. With this end in view,
they have thought that they could turn to good account the difficulties of the evolutionary apologetic and the doubtfulness as-
cribed to universal principles on the basis of the modern study
of history. They decided that nothing could be done with the
concept of a universal principle of religion, for at every point
it ran afoul of the historical particular and was of no avail in
reaching a normative principle. Therefore, the normative, they
said, was not to be found on the broad basis of some lowest common denominator but could only be obtained on the narrow
basis of a phenomenon that was utterly unique and individual.
This narrow basis was then said to be provided by Christianity
because of its limitation to a historically unique figure and to a
specific way of accounting for its sense of certainty.

Some members of the Ritschlian school next proceed to argue that what constitutes the individual uniqueness of Christianity is the claim it makes to absolute truth and the redemption effected by means of this absolute truth. Scholars engaged in the scientific study and evaluation of Christianity are supposed to accommodate themselves to this uniqueness by taking the claim that isolates Christianity from, and opposes it to, every other religion and adopting it as a presupposition of their work. This presupposition is then confirmed by considerations of a general nature which bring Christianity into relationship, first, with the thoroughly natural postulates of the moral man and, second, with the corresponding intimations of these postulates in the non-Christian religions. Christianity is thus the highest conceivable religion, since it satisfies the natural moral postulates and also fulfills the suggestions of general revelation found outside Christianity.

Another line of argument begins by restricting the scientific study of religion solely to a phenomenological psychology of mechanistic causation. At the same time, however, it is also held that the normative must reveal itself in one particular historical religion which—and this is especially important—by means of an absolute revelation of the spirit of moral freedom breaks through the causal processes that otherwise apply. Such a religion must necessarily exist. Christianity proves that it is precisely such a religion, for it is unique in claiming that a revelation and a redemption of this kind exist in Jesus and that this claim is brought to realization by the forcefulness of the impression Jesus makes on us. The legitimacy of this claim is confirmed, these theologians contend, by its congruence with the moral postulates of the natural consciousness. Thus they arrive at a unique and explicitly Christian certainty which is fulfilled in personal decision and which makes it possible to discern a motivating power of God in the psychological impulses at work in non-Christian religious beliefs as well as to find a criterion of judgment distinct from them.[2]

Other members of this school may proceed along somewhat different lines, but invariably there is a "Christian epistemology" based on the impossibility of making use of a universal principle of religion as well as on the impossibility of obtaining a criterion of value from such a principle. This epistemology takes its criterion in the first instance from Christianity's "individual and historical" claim to absolute revelation and redemption, but also from the confirmation of this claim suggested by its congruence with the natural moral consciousness.

It is obvious, however, that this is only toying with the concept of what it means for something to be historical and individual. According to the view of the Ritschlian school, there is no denying the possibility that the individual uniqueness which exists in the "natural" consciousness and in the non-Christian religions can be understood in terms of the universal principle of general and natural revelation. At the same time, however, the concept of the historical and individual, which refers to phenomena subject to the unique conditions of a given time, is supposed to prove that the Christian religion is supra-individual absolute truth by giving emphasis to the claim Christianity makes for itself. In the first instance the concept of individuality does infinitely less than is necessary, in the second infinitely more than is justified. Under the heading of opposition to the concept of a universal principle of religion, together with stress on the historical and individual, what we actually have here is simply the old antithesis between Christianity and everything non-Christian. By the use of these ideas, everything non-Christian is instantly brought into conformity with that way of thinking which sees other religions in terms of natural revelations and postulates of universal scope, while Christianity is understood in terms of supernatural absolute revelation. This absolute, supernatural revelation, however, remains in a curious state of suspense, for it is absoluteness without the form of absoluteness, i.e., without a defining concept of miraculous causality and without a complete, authenticating realization of the principle of religion. On the contrary, Jesus and primitive Christianity are always regarded both as absolute and also as individual historical phenomena in the genuine meaning of the term, i.e., as phenomena conditioned by their period of history. This means not only that they are phenomena to be investigated with critical discrimination and historical techniques but also that they are believed to have undergone radical changes in their subsequent historical development. Thus this obscure and undefined "absoluteness" is constantly in conflict with the simultaneously acknowledged historical character of Christianity.

Further tracing of historical interconnections reveals, moreover, the close ties that join Christianity and the non-Christian religions, ties that contradict the allegedly absolute gulf between them. If the historical horizon is extended a bit more, one encounters the analogous claims of other religions, claims that are just as intrinsic to their nature as the Christian claim is to Christianity. At that point, some would substantiate the Christian claim by virtue of its congruity with the postulates of the natural consciousness, but to the writer these postulates themselves appear as products of history. They derive from a reality in which men put their trust and are connected with Christianity to the extent that the level of religious sensitivity in a given religion makes it a practical approximation of Christianity. In their purest form, indeed, these postulates are today historical products of Christianity, and they continue to exert influence, even though the theologian may suppose they do not find satisfaction in Christian salvation and even though the doubter may have lost his faith.

Thus this school with its emphasis on the historical—which is at the same time a denial of the consequences of what it means to be historical—leads to the formulation of increasingly acute historical questions, yet also to an increasingly radical undercutting of its own basis in history. Hence it is this school that has given rise to the method of procedure that was followed in this section of our inquiry, namely, taking another look at the old liberal theology in order to reexamine the basic concepts of the idealistic evolutionary apologetic, which alone has taken universal historical thought seriously.

3

HISTORICAL
RELATIVITY
AND
NORMS
OF
VALUE

The foregoing reexamination was primarily concerned with the attempt to prove from the history of evolution that Christianity is the absolute religion because of its congruity with the principle of religion. Our conclusion was, to be sure, a negative one. Positively expressed, this conclusion might read as follows: The Christian religion is in every moment of its history a purely historical phenomenon, subject to all the limitations to which any individual historical phenomenon is exposed, just like the other great religions. It is to be investigated, in every moment of its history, by the universal, verified methods of historical research. Just as these methods demonstrate their fruitfulness in relation to Christianity, so too do they confirm, when applied to Christianity, their general presuppositions as to the nature of everything historical. To employ the methods without their substantive presuppositions would be to use a lever without a fulcrum. If the lever of historical method has raised the level of our understanding of Christian history, then by so doing it has also demonstrated that the fulcrum of a universally historical mode of thinking is true. If one should wish to say "Christianity is a relative phenomenon," there is no reason to object to this, for the historical and the relative are identical. Acknowledgment of this proposition can be evaded only by one who has deliberately or instinctively thrown up a bulwark to defend Christianity from the modern study of history.

There can be no doubt about this result. However, it is by no means shocking. Only the misguided thought habits of rational or supernatural dogmatism surround the word "relative" with all the terrors of the uncertain, the unstable, the purposeless. What everything really depends on is what the concept "relative" means and how it relates to the problem of acquiring criteria of value. We have already given an exact definition of the concept of the absolute; we must now discuss the concept of historical relativity and its relationship to the attaining of norms.[1]

It appears to many that the inevitable consequence of historical thinking is an unlimited relativism. History, in this view, takes certain temporarily related elements and produces a transitory uniqueness, and since this is a repetitive process, it means that history itself turns into an incalculable welter of evanescent forms. There are three reasons for believing that historical thinking has this effect.

First, as soon as analytical specialization takes over, it divides independent phenomena into smaller ones for the sake of more exact research and thus acquires an immeasurable minuteness of detail. Such depiction of details does indeed appear, like a roaring ocean of trivial relativities, to swallow up every existing meaning and purpose in history.

In the second place is the naturalistic mode of derivation and explanation. According to this approach, all phenomena are to be treated deductively as necessary consequences of their antecedents and environment since, as a matter of fact, every phenomenon stands in a demonstrable relationship to both. But the moment such a view permits the helm of the idealistic concept of evolution to slip out of its hand, it is tossed on a restless sea of endless historical configurations which constantly appear and disappear, intersect and overlap like the structures found in nature. Only a fortunate combination of circumstances permits such configurations to enjoy a comparatively long existence. Here, then, there is nothing really *new* and hence no transcending of the pure givenness of nature with its endless interplay of already existent forces.

Third, the art of hypothetical empathy for heterogeneous

forms including both their internal and external presuppositions —an art fundamental to historical understanding—has resulted in an unlimited virtuosity in the changing of standpoints from which judgments can be formed. The rationale for this changing of standpoints is that everything is to be understood and appraised in and of itself alone. But as a result, historical impartiality seems guilty not so much of letting its light shine on the righteous and unrighteous alike but of no longer recognizing this distinction at all. Weak natures thus identify the modern idea of history with appreciation for alien things but with denial of one's own heritage; they identify it with skepticism and intellectual dabbling, or with a blasé attitude and lack of faith.

Such failings, however, are by no means intrinsic to historical thinking and have indeed been firmly rejected by the great representatives of this mode of thought. First of all, specialization, in this connection, is nothing but a perhaps unavoidable shortsightedness or, if it persists, a meaningless duplication of reality. All scientific study of history, on the other hand, makes use of detailed studies only as a means; it never regards them as an ultimate end. And they are indeed means to the understanding of the great, self-contained civilizations, the leading nations, and important dimensions and branches of culture. Comprehensive syntheses of this kind require both detailed preliminary studies and the overall mastery of great historians, and they will continue to require them as long as such syntheses constitute the sole purpose for which history is studied. That scholars capable of such synthesis are rare, like Newton and Helmholtz in the natural sciences, is beside the point. Not everybody can conceive of and write authentic history, and the modern notion that everyone who has a little technical training is a historian is nothing but a disease of our age. Much that goes under the name of history-writing today is not history but the work of amateurs; far from being history, it is, rather, clay for the bricks with which history is built.

In the same way, secondly, deductions and explanations of a causal-mechanistic kind are by no means to be thought of as intrinsic to the historical way of thinking. Deductive, mechanistic explanations make everything internal dependent on impinging external influences and deny everything new and creative. But that is only transferring the method of natural science, with its quest for universal laws, into the dimension of history. The result is that something essential drops out of history, namely, the individual and unique. Coming into existence in the interaction of given forces, what is individual and unique is by no means derivable from known antecedents but emerges from the transcendent depths of history and comes to actualization in relation to the given. What is unique and individual is, in a word, a new creation. Even if a particular historical complex seems to be characterized by an overall uniformity because of the comparatively weak individual uniqueness of its members, nevertheless the complex itself is something unique, something characterized by points of departure that are by nature highly individual. Even if the physical infrastructure—geographical, anthropological, and economic interrelations—has the effect of producing a matrix of uniform conditions, what is historically important is the individual reaction that follows from the unique character of men and nations. The more this reaction gives rise to enduring moral strength for the overcoming of such natural conditions, the more its significance increases. Thus in the modern study of history there can be no question of an endless accumulation of discrete, spontaneously organizing and disorganizing forces. We have to do, rather, with substantive components and principles of life that take shape in the depths of the soul and then rise to a place alongside the natural structures that condition and serve human need. Such components and principles are not mere products of antecedents or environment but are creative regulators of historical life. Their claims to validity are based not on the causal necessity of their origin but upon their truth. Our thinking about causation is too much under the influence of a naturalistic scholasticism—which is, after all, just as much of a scholasticism as the dialectic of the Hegelian school or an ecclesiastical philosophy that has substituted a theory of miracle for Aristotelianism. Understanding of history has to be drawn from history itself and, to the extent that history must be transcended, from epistemology as well as from a philosophy of culture and metaphysics based on this epistemology; it is not to be drawn from the natural sciences.[2]

In the third and last place, historical impartiality and hypothetical empathy are not at all well adapted to supporting a meaningless, purposeless relativism. Behind these attitudes is the idea that every man is a microcosm, capable of acquiring an understanding of the nature and function of apparently alien situations because of definite points of correspondence between them and himself. This means, therefore, that the different value orientations of mankind have something in common. It is this common factor that impels us to compare and contrast the values they embody and, further, to establish criteria and form judgments about human history—just as we do about individual personalities—on the basis of the conclusions arrived at in the course of such comparative assessment. If one is no longer aware of such an urge, he has simply fallen prey to weakness or disintegration of ethical discernment or despair over a religious faith that guarantees a unified goal of things. It is no accident that people like Renan reach a dead end as theologians before they work out their peculiar understandings of history.

Thus all these notions that make the idea of relativity so repellent to us are by no means necessarily bound to it. Relativity simply means that all historical phenomena are unique, individual configurations acted on by influences from a universal context that comes to bear on them in varying degrees of immediacy. It means, therefore, that every independent structure leads one to a perspective that embraces broader and still broader horizons till finally it opens out onto the whole. It means that a comprehensive perspective of this kind allows one to form universal judgments and evaluations. Relativity does not mean, however, denial of the values that appear in these individual configurations, that are oriented in the same direction, that have the power to encounter and influence one another, and that as a result of such interaction lead men to discern their inner truth and necessity and thus make a choice among them. At every moment of history these values partake of the peculiarities of the situation to which they belong. Even the forming of a conception of these values, not to mention forming judgments about them, can take place only in ways conditioned by a given historical moment. Absolute, unchanging value, conditioned by nothing temporal, exists not within but beyond history and can be perceived only in presentiment and faith.

The scientific study of history does not exclude norms. On the contrary, its most important task is that of discerning norms and striving to see them as a unified whole. But the norms themselves, as well as the ways they are conceptually unified, remain individual and temporally conditioned entities throughout every moment of their existence. They always represent a situationally informed striving toward a future goal, a goal that is not yet completely realized and has not yet become absolute.

The problem faced by the modern approach to history is not that of making an either/or choice between relativism and absolutism but that of how to combine the two. This is the problem of how to discern, in the relative, tendencies toward the absolute goal. Or, to state the problem more accurately: How does one work out a fresh, durable, and creative synthesis that will give the absolute the form possible to it at a particular moment and yet remain true to its inherent limitation as a mere approximation of true, ultimate, and universally valid values? That is the nub of the problem, and it cannot be set aside either by the naturalization of history or by skeptically oriented specialization. It arises directly out of the material of history itself.

Since the course proposed here is one that leads from historical description as such to taking a position toward value orientations that appear within history, the limits of descriptive history and therewith of history in its primary and narrower meaning are of course transcended. However, if this position is not predetermined by speculative, metaphysical norms or by supernatural, dogmatic standards smuggled in from other contexts, then all determination of rank and value among these orientations must relate directly to, and arise from, the findings to which historical research leads, much in the same way that descriptive history itself depends on evaluation which, even if expressed only occasionally, materially determines the spirit of the description as a whole. All that is required is that the position one takes be developed with the necessary comprehensiveness of perspective and with the necessary clarity as to its conditions and presuppositions.

Thus the modern study of history gives rise to a task that is always associated with it and is indeed its ultimate responsibility, namely, to work out a synthesis and evaluation that will form the nucleus of a philosophy of history. In the execution of this task only the outstanding forms of religious development need be taken directly into consideration. The important thing is to compare these developments in such a way as to take in the widest possible historical horizon in the hope of discerning not a universal principle of law like that at work in concepts employed in the natural sciences but a principle suggestive of tendencies toward a common goal.

This does not mean that we will now survey the total development of mankind and, on the basis of this concept of a common goal, patch together a theory which we recognize in advance will be impracticable due to our fragmentary knowledge and the impossibility of making history conform to our theoretical demands for laws. What it does mean is that we will draw together the most outstanding results of man's spiritual development that are known and accessible to us, basing this procedure on the supposition that their being known to us is not a mere accident but is due to the fact that they are the only significant developments which spring from an elemental matrix.

One can, it is true, have reservations about this supposition. The presence of man on the earth must be calculated, at the very least, in several hundreds of thousands of years, and we are familiar, to a certain extent, with only the last six or seven thousand. How long man will continue to exist on our planet is quite unknown, but it can no doubt be reckoned in similar periods of time. In addition, the climatic changes associated with the shifting of the poles in the Ice Ages brought about great changes in the physical foundations of culture. It is not in itself impossible, therefore, that our history might have had a predecessor and that its tradition was utterly obliterated. However, we need not be led astray by what is completely unknown, whether in the past or in the future. We must concentrate on the world of culture that is known to us, and this world entitles us, because of the combination of generic unity and individual distinctiveness it exhibits, to assume that every present or future ascent of man in the scale of civilization will develop along essentially similar lines.

So we are left with the task of drawing together and analyzing what has emerged within the horizons of the world as it presently exists and the more or less clearly known history that it embraces. Thus the modern study of history leads to the task of comparing the major forms of religious orientation from a single, inclusive perspective, and this places a new and even more extensive restriction on relativism.

This point may be clarified by some further considerations.

First of all, it would be highly fallacious to think of historical relativism as if it involved a limitless number of competing values. On the contrary, experience shows that such values are exceedingly few in number and that disclosures of really new goals for the human spirit are rare indeed. Only at the lower levels of culture does unlimited multiplicity exist, and this is simply a multiplicity of externals or forms that signifies, in actuality, a stark monotony. Not till we come to the higher stages do there appear great, formative powers of the inner life, and breakthroughs to these stages are by no means numerous. Those who really have something new to say to men are exceptionally rare, and it is astonishing that man lives, in fact, by so few ideas. Thus in the history of religions in particular, we find ourselves confronted not by a profusion of powerful religious forces, among which we would never be able to choose, but only by a few great orientations.

Polytheism and the numerous religions of uncivilized peoples are irrelevant to the problem of highest religious values. As for religions of ethical and spiritual greatness, which posit a higher world in antithesis to the merely given world of physical and psychological nature, we find only a limited number. The ones to be taken into consideration here are, on the one hand, the religions that sprang from a common stock—Judaism, Christianity, and Islam—and, on the other, the great religions of the East, namely, Hinduism and especially Buddhism. Also important are the philosophical attempts to sever every connection with history and create a purely rational religion in terms of monistic pantheism, dualistic mysticism, or moralistic theism. The ones to be considered here are the great schools of ethico-religious speculation that began with Platonism in late antiquity, Indian philosophy of religion, and also the modern revivals of these philosophical systems. As regards these various orientations, however, a starting point in the history of religions forces us to make an even greater simplification.

In the first place, the rational religions are in every instance only offshoots of the positive, historical religions, and for all their speculative subtlety, in no case do they possess a strong, independent, religious impulse. From them proceeds neither religious power nor religious community, even though, as in the case of Platonism and Stoicism, they did help prepare the way for a new religious awakening and even though, as in the case of the scientifically influenced religious spirit of the modern period, they are capable of modifying the dominant religions. The creative power of religion pulses only in the historical religions, and every attempt to work out a position with regard to the religious values of mankind must begin with them. That is why the philosophy of religion of late antiquity has maintained an indissoluble tie with Christianity up to the present day, and why Indian speculation finds its support in Hinduism and Buddhism. In the same way all modern philosophical religions are actuated by identical impulses and contain absolutely no new religious idea or power. The field narrows down, therefore, to the rivalry between three or four basic orientations in which the power of religion is disclosed, orientations that have their counterpart in, and give support to, entire spheres of culture. Indeed, it is not too much to say that essentially we have to do with the rivalry between the prophetic, Christian, Platonic, and Stoic world of ideas on the one hand, and the Buddhist or Eastern world of ideas on the other.

In the second place, acknowledgment of the relativity of all historical phenomena does not rightly include the demand that these dynamic configurations be regarded as only temporarily influential but destined to disappear. There is nothing to prevent us from regarding the significant results of scientific, political, artistic, social, and religious life as enduring. It must be remembered, however, that just as these results took shape within definite contexts, so too they always assume individual forms. The doctrine of endless progress, or rather the theory of endless change, is a groundless prejudgment that seems plausible only to people who have consigned all metaphysical ideas regarding a transcendent background of history to the status of illusion—and with such ideas the religious belief in the unity and meaningfulness of reality. Of itself, historical thinking by no means necessitates such nihilism. On the contrary, when one recalls how few great orientations history has thus far brought forth and the extent and tenacity of their influence, it seems highly improbable that the future will suddenly begin to turn out more of them in a chaotic and confusing productivity. It is far more likely that the ascent to the highlands will now be followed by expansion over the plateau, that the future will bring struggle and encounter, further development and enrichment of already existing potentialities—as long, at least, as the continuity of our culture endures. What is of chief importance in this connection is the victory of the highest values and the incorporation of all reality into their frame of reference. Determinative at every point, therefore, is ethically oriented religious faith that includes the idea of an end, and this is something no scientific imagination can give. The assurance thus provided by faith need fear none of the effects of historical relativism. Just as man has developed into a definite sort of being biologically, so too his religious, or more broadly his cultural, nature has already been disclosed so far as its principal features are concerned. No superman of some previously unimagined type is to be expected.

In the third place, the historical way of thinking by no means excludes the possibility of comparing the most important elements and values of the main religious orientations, ranking them in accordance with a criterion of value, and subsuming them under the idea of a common goal. Though transcending history in its changeless perfection, this goal can be manifested within history at different points along the ascent toward the higher orientations of life in ways adapted to each historical situation and its presuppositions. These different manifestations can be measured and compared with one another as regards the simplicity, depth, and power with which they disclose a higher, transcendent life in God. The faith in God that lives in every higher religion demands at least that much comparison. Comparative evaluation of this kind, however, belongs to the very nature of historical thinking and is also suggested by experience. For historical thinking would be incapable of the hypothetical empathy its task requires if there did not come to expression in all historical forms something of the ideals we ourselves hold or that we, by entering into them, might learn to recognize as our own. Experience shows, as a matter of fact, that at every stage of religious development the ultimate problems of life are characterized in essentially similar ways, and that in the teachings of the great religious leaders similar solutions appear. On every hand the purposive character of life, which transcends the senses and the world, comes out into the open and reveals its battle against a life totally bound to the conditions of natural existence. The differences between religions, apart from those attributable to unique historical conditions, exist only in the depth, power, and clarity with which the higher life is revealed.

The criterion by which these differences are to be weighed cannot, of course, be a theory of religion deduced *a priori* from some place or other, nor can it be a concept of what is empirically common to these religions considered as a class. Contemporary thought is no longer able to start with pure reason, while a mere abstracting of empirical regularities would draw together only lowest common denominators and overlook the salient and really decisive features of the whole. It is only in the free interaction of ideas that the criterion can take shape. By involvement in the great struggles of mankind, by hypothetically entering into the various competing orientations, one must always, in both a personal and practical way, appropriate and experience the criterion anew. No longer is it to be found in the self-evident truth of the idea by which one's own sphere of culture is controlled, this idea being regarded as ordained by God himself. That was how the Middle Ages understood it. Nor is it to be found in an atemporal, ahistorical, spontaneous reason that engenders identical knowledge in every individual if he only gives the matter sufficient thought. That was how the Enlightenment understood it. In the same way that we today think of the ultimate primarily as an inexhaustible movement of life, we may likewise understand the criterion of evaluation as something that emerges within this movement of life as a result of a universal perspective on the one hand, and involvement in this movement on the other. It can be characterized as the determining of a direction, the setting of a course among the great, dominant tendencies of history. The criterion itself is both the product of a particular historical situation and a means for its further development; it is not a static and completed principle that determines how the process will take place.

Since revelations that depend on personality become increasingly significant as one goes up the scale of religions, while what the individual person can produce in the area of religion becomes less and less important, we cannot regard the criterion as an entity that hangs in midair above the historical religions but as something that requires us to choose among them in a process of free development. The criterion will emerge from the religion that is strongest and most profound, appropriating from the others only what has been worked out with particular effectiveness. It must be rooted in a positive, historical religion, and it must teach us, by reference to the principle of comparison, to set aside many things that, in the absence of such comparison, previously stood in the foreground, and to give stronger emphasis to many things that formerly blended into the background.

Such a criterion is, then, a matter of personal conviction and is in the last analysis admittedly subjective. However, there is no other way to obtain a criterion that will enable us to choose among competing historical values. It is, in short, a personal, ethically oriented, religious conviction acquired by comparison and evaluation. In situations where the unquestioned dominance of a given outlook has been broken and where rivalry between different historical forces for a fresh understanding of the situation has been initiated or where actual encounter has begun, there is no other choice. It has its objective basis in a scrupulous survey of the major religious orientations, in unprejudiced hypothetical empathy, and in conscientious evaluation, but its ultimate determination remains a matter of personal, subjective, inner conviction. For this reason not every theory-spinner who comes along is capable of this kind of work, but only thinkers who combine profound and extensive knowledge with serious ethical and religious concern. Not everybody need attack and solve this problem anew; only those are called who actually have a profound and penetrating perception of the problem and who possess the ethical resoluteness necessary for its solution. The inner truth and force of their solution will convince others. Most important, choices among competing value orientations must not be made in a realm of theoretical abstraction inhabited only by the thoughts of a few European scholars and savants. They must be hammered out in ever widening circles and in actual confrontation between religions. Here judgments that seem pleasing in theory will have to prove themselves in practice.

For all its subjectivity the criterion is, therefore, by no means fortuitous. It is not as if it arose as a mere extension of a traditionally dominant mentality, nor is it a mere opinion—set forth in a thousand variations—of separate persons who must each conceive the world anew out of his own head and then proceed to the task of evaluation. The notion that because of the fallaciousness of all previous solutions to the problems of life everyone must now detect the value of things in the most capricious or contradictory forms is fully as morbid and over-individualistic a misconception of the great idea of autonomy as is the fear that the world, hitherto shot through so magnificently with ideal forces, will be reduced to a lifeless web or a senseless chaos as a result of the demand for impartiality. As over against such notions, it is of the very essence of historical thinking to mark out clearly the great value orientations that have been achieved in the course of history and by which our existence is upheld, and to look into the depths of their interrelationship. Independent, ongoing, constructive work of this kind contains more inner strength and freedom than the willingness to mix everything with the quicksand of fantasies that merely reflect the supposition that for everything that exists and is believed in, the converse could quite as easily be possible.

If, however, comparison of value orientations leads to the forming of a criterion of judgment, then this very fact shows both that these structures are comparable and that they are related to something *common and universally valid* within them. This common element, however, is not a general principle abstracted from factual correspondences, nor is it the more limited idea that what should be abstracted is not a law common to all historical life but only that which inheres in the higher religious and ethical forms of thought. It is a matter, rather, of identifying the orienting *goals and ideals* that find individually conditioned realization in every form of life but are fully realized in none, that simply accompany and give direction to the process of realization as its ultimate end or purpose. By correlation and comparison the basic features of this dynamic process become apparent and differentiate the various orientations from one another. The converging lines evident in these basic features suggest, however, a normative, universally valid goal toward which the whole is directed. The nature of this goal can be known, despite the considerable diversity of its individual preparatory forms, while the idea that infuses it, discernible on every hand, permits the forming of judgments as to the degree of its realization. This normative and universally valid goal, considered as something perfect and complete, lies beyond history. Within history it can only be apprehended, at any given time, in forms that are by nature individual and conditioned.

In these diverse perceptions of the ultimate goal toward which man is oriented there exists, then, a natural gradation based on the greater or, as the case may be, more limited strength and clarity of the revelation of the higher life. From this gradation arises the expectation that the goal-directed impetus existing in this idea of an ultimate objective may lead to a revelation that is in principle definitive and final. Of course every new stage in the revelatory process must for its part stand as a historically constituted realization and precursor of the ultimate goal of man, and to that extent it is, as Ranke was fond of saying, "directly related to God." At the same time, however, each stage also affords a foundation essential to all further development. The point is to work out on this basis increasingly extensive and penetrating— if always individual and temporally conditioned—explications of the goal toward which mankind is directed.

Such a philosophy of history admittedly leads, in the last analysis, to the question of the ultimate end and to that of the participation of the individual in that end. It leads, that is to say, to questions that cannot be answered without the concept of something that lies beyond earthly history. These are questions, however, about which each of us has equally much and equally little to say. They may be left, therefore, as far as this inquiry is concerned, to the postulates and inferences that people venture to project out of the present into the future.

If we get this far, it may be that we will have reached the principle of normativeness and universal validity which is both common to all religions and at the same time absolute. It should be remembered, however, that this is not an actual universal which is exhausted in its human realization. It is the concept, rather, of a common, orienting goal that may from time to time manifest itself in history in clear and distinct preparatory forms but always remains a goal "out in front." A goal of this kind can be a common one and yet never really be grasped except in an individual and historical way. In a given historical phenomenon it may find itself embodied in a preliminary form that gives powerful and concentrated expression to all its converging tendencies; still, it will not have been exhausted in this phenomenon but will only have found in it a clarity that in principle constantly seeks expression in new forms. It remains a common goal but not a law or universal principle of phenomena. What is required is a definitive disclosure of its main direction but not an absolute realization. And even that disclosure need not be limited by any kind of theoretical necessity to any one, single point. Instead, the forces generated at the various points of disclosure or break-through tend to converge. As applied to religion, what is suggested is not a "principle" of religion as a humanly realizable and exhaustible idea, but the concept of a goal discernible in outline and general direction. What is suggested is the concept of a goal that always remains transcendent as far as the sum total of its content is concerned, a goal that can be apprehended within history only in individually conditioned ways.

In psychological and epistemological perspective, what is normative and universally valid thus appears as the concept of a goal toward which mankind is directed. The goal itself, however, is simply set before man as a higher reality, a creative personal reality that breaks forth out of the human spirit and has its basis in the unconditioned worth of the inner man. It is this reality that provides the creative force at work in man's conception of a goal, his forward-driving restlessness and yearning, his resistance to the merely natural world. This idea requires *a turn to the metaphysical,* a retracing of all man's goals and orientations to a transcendent force that actuates our deepest strivings and is connected with the creative core of reality. The various eruptions, breakthroughs, and manifestations of the higher spiritual life are rooted in the goal-oriented character of this force. It stands over against what is merely given in nature and towers up at different points—here clearly and profoundly, there more weakly and obscurely—till it has found concentrated expression, from that point on pressing forward to goals that exceed all knowledge and imagination. This is the permanent element in the *concept of evolutionary development,* which in this case signifies not only a postulate that accompanies all faith in the spiritual life but also a fact of experience that has been manifested with some degree of clarity.

To be sure, the attempt to identify this concept of a goal with a generative, causal law has to be abandoned; so too with the attempt to compute absolute realization from an empirical series of qualitative gradations and from what is alleged to be a historically demonstrable exhausting of its inner principle. The doctrine that stages of development can be calculated according to a strict law—the Hegelian dialectic—has to be given up. We also have to relinquish the correlated doctrine of the pure and exhaustive explication of the idea in the phenomenon, by virtue of which every unique and transient form is understood both as a refractory concealment and a communication of the absolute idea, this paradoxicality being deemed essential to the developmental process of realization. It must not be maintained that reality is panlogistic and monistic in character. Just as what is universally valid is not a law that calls the whole of reality into being, so evolutionary development is not mere successive realization of an idea. Evolutionary development means, rather, the eruption—at coexisting but discrete points—of dynamic orientations directed toward the absolute goal of the human spirit. Each orientation evolves the richness of the potential granted to it, first in its own limited sphere. At length these orientations come into contact with one another. Then in free religious and ethical encounter men take note of their gradations of value and strive to obtain a basis of judgment by drawing them together to form a philosophy of history.

Seen from this angle, all such dynamic orientations are temporally conditioned, individual phenomena. They do not take what derives from the idea and refine it into a pure and universal principle. By means of constantly new, situationally correlated involvements, they give it unique and individual shapes. Consequently, they always have to reckon with purely elemental underlying conditions, contingent circumstances, and hostile resistance to the idea. If, among these orientations, there should occur a breakthrough capable in principle of giving focused expression to them all, even this could only be an individual historical event. It could do no more than disentangle its idea-derived elements from their previous forms and connections, and then introduce them ever and again into equally individual contexts.

Out of the infinitely rich and mobile whole of reality one can indeed abstract particular facets. One can isolate its universally regular elements as laws of nature and establish the individuality of its historical configurations in the network of interrelationships they form. One cannot, however, recombine these two into a unified organic development according to which both the necessity of the sequence and the value gradations of the stages might be abstracted from one uniform law of the whole. This notion, popular even today due to the influence of Hegel, is not practicable in this form. The speculative concept of evolution remains an intuition and a presentiment. Science can establish causal relationships only from case to case, while from another angle, it can only construe the conditions necessary for forming a criterion of value. The criterion itself, however, remains the creation of a historical moment and is also a means of advancing toward the future. It cannot be reliably inferred from a universal law of evolution; it is, rather, an intimation of such a law, an intimation governed by the criterion that takes shape within a concrete situation.

In the application of the concept of evolution as it is understood here, the *history of religions* has a special role to play.[3] The state, society, art, science—indeed, all the substantive components of culture—clearly represent values and principles that are in themselves quite objective and valid. These values and principles do not proceed from subjective desires but disclose a new and higher world. Yet even though they thus suggest that the foundation and coherence of this world depend on a higher, spiritual reality and to that extent always contain an element of religion, they are directed toward forms of natural reality that are perpetually changing and evolving new relationships. For that reason these values and principles, despite the simplicity of their underlying ideas, are constantly exposed to new complexities at critical turning points. Religion, however, in the stricter sense of elevation to the divine in religious experience, is directed, conversely, to the eternal and abiding. Precisely for this reason, religion stands in a comparatively tense relationship with all culture, even though culture has its ultimate presupposition and support in religion. By the same reasoning, culture participates in an immediate, inner presence of the divine that is not always easily discernible in mundane reality or in human activity.

This immediate, inner presence of the divine and this relationship to the eternal and abiding ground of all spiritual life, then, not only undergird the utter simplicity of the religious idea but also make it inconceivable that this elemental and highly concentrated nucleus of life should be exposed to violent fluctuations or manifested in a large number of revelations. If this substantive component of culture is already relatively simple and constant in all its most important tendencies, it follows that the religious idea and its power become completely evident in only a few great revelations. This justifies the expectation that its essential meaning is disclosed in the upward movement of human history and not at some point of roaring confusion that would in all likelihood be quite alien to us.

Consequently, the more we hold to the conviction that the most important components of culture have already come into existence and that they provide us with unlimited possibilities of application, the less do we need to think it shortsighted or naïve if, when it comes to religion, we believe that it has already disclosed its content to us in principle and that what is now called for is the achieving of unity and coherence in the spiritual life on the basis of this point of reference. As the great themes of human endeavor have everywhere been worked out in the upward course of history, it is even more certain that the religious principle has found its essential clarity in this upward movement. What is to be expected from the few great breakthroughs of the religious principle, therefore, is not the aimless vagary of a multiplicity of revelations but the victory of the purest and most profound idea of God.

As the history of religions shows, this idea of God is not to be sought in some kind of scientistic religion or in a general principle of religion that abstracts only what the various religions hold in common and for that reason overlooks their important differences. It is to be sought, rather, among the *positive, historical, religious orientations and revelations.*

Within culture generally, really new developments are exceptional. Individual differentiation proceeds by building on the basic structures that have already come into existence, whereas the activity of individual persons in creating something genuinely new tends to diminish. This is the case in even higher degree in the realm of religion.[4] As history advances, the creative religious powers of individual persons become more and more limited precisely because the religious orientations themselves become increasingly profound and forceful. The religious strivings of individuals come to be more and more concerned with appropriating the great revelations, while individual piety finds itself able to add only nuances of tone and understanding. The religious weakness and debility, the desire for redemption and surrender found in all the higher religions are simply the obverse side of the enhanced goals and powers of religion. They are evidence that in the higher religions the individual can no longer create religious orientations or ideas at will. It is for this reason that in the upward movement of history the specifically religious life becomes differentiated from the more general spiritual and cultural setting. Energetic and one-sided religious personalities stand out with increasing clarity as the source of all religious orientations, and from them alone the transforming power of great religious movements proceeds.

This is overlooked by modern relativists and individualists who believe that in view of the exposure of previously influential religious illusions, the time has now come for religions of books and pamphlets, in which everyone appeals to the historical relativism that has at last been discovered and that he can even augment with his own fabrications of religion. Yet it is such people as these who have signally failed to understand the lesson of history. History shows that it is the more highly evolved type of religion that, for reasons intrinsic to its nature, remains bound to historical reality. It pursues its course not by nullifying this reality but by extending, elaborating, and refining it. Our world of culture, and least of all our science, which is naturally becoming increasingly diversified, will never produce a "new religion," for such a religion could emerge only out of the depths of a naïve and vigorous ethos simultaneously suffused with the highest of ideals. We will have to rely on the great religious orientations as they presently exist, defending them from the cultural diseases of skepticism and anarchy on the one hand, while attuning them to new intellectual horizons and accommodating them to new socio-ethical tasks on the other.[5]

The results of the modern study of history lead to considerations of this nature. Such considerations belong, admittedly, to the philosophy of history and to that extent are not scientific in the strict sense. Science, however, does not mean exact science alone. Otherwise it would have to be confined to mathematics and natural science—and perhaps to historical research based strictly on motivational psychology. The most important tasks of science, as far as the inner life is concerned, lie, rather, in a sphere that does not lend itself to exactness and strictness in this sense for the reason that practical, subjective valuations and attitudes are involved at every turn. In this sphere every attempt to rule out the contributory role of such factors and to apply the methods of the natural or exact sciences has led only to absurdity and the renunciation of any knowledge of consequence.

Conversely, this sphere cannot be relinquished to that approach which rejects scientific reflection. This approach has itself long stood under scientific influence, but what it took over from science was adopted uncritically without being thought out to the end. As a result, it constantly vacillates between naïve prejudices and anarchistic skepticism.

The only course that remains, therefore, is the kind of scientific inquiry in which men strive as best they can to comprehend empirical, historical reality and to acquire norms from history by conscientious comparison and reflection. The study of history is not of itself the obtaining of such norms but the ground from which they arise. Historically delineated and actual norms are not necessarily norms we should acknowledge as valid for ourselves; they are disclosures of that principle from which we evolve valid norms.

Two propositions belong to the presuppositions of a philosophy of history and constitute the primary underlying subjective elements out of which all else arises. One deals with norms generally and consists of an acknowledgment that the human spirit is intended to abide by the norms of a binding higher reality. The other expresses the confidence that all the norms thus manifested will ultimately coalesce in a final, unitary idea of absolute necessity and value which, being ultimate, will remain eternally transcendent in relation to history and yet stand before us as our orienting goal and ideal.

History is a unique sphere of knowledge because it is the sphere of the individual and nonrecurrent. But within the individual and nonrecurrent, there is something universally valid— or something connected with the universally valid—which makes itself known at the same time. The problem is to hold these two elements together in the right relation. The Enlightenment fixed its gaze on the universal and valid. German idealism, with poetic absorption—and with some justification—perceived multiplicity on every hand and, to the extent that it sought in vain to control multiplicity by its metaphysical theory of evolution, opened the door to the unlimited relativism of the present day. The Enlightenment conception stood closer to the basic urgings of the human ethos and perceived the main tendencies of history perhaps more correctly than much modern study of history with its concern for the microscopic. On the other hand, the discoveries made by the modern study of history have presented us with a world full of depth, richness, and vitality. This world seems far truer and more alive to us than that found in the Enlightenment idea of history. Thus the problem is to define the scope of the relative and individual with ever increasing exactness and to understand with ever increasing comprehensiveness the universally valid that works teleologically within history. Then we will see that the relative contains an indication of the unconditional. In the relative we will find a token of the absolute that transcends history. Goethe once put it thus:

> "Admission denied to the land of ideas"?
> But I guess I know its strand.
> One who cannot gain the isle
> May anchor off the land.

4

CHRISTIANITY: FOCAL POINT AND CULMINATION OF ALL RELIGIOUS DEVELOPMENTS

Let us formulate the conclusion suggested by this inquiry so far.

The historical way of thinking does not preclude our acknowledging Christianity as the highest religious truth that has relevance for us, a truth on the basis of which an evaluative understanding rooted in religious faith and developed with reference to the religions of the world might be organized. That, in a nutshell, is how the outcome of our considerations can be formulated. This formulation, however, leaves unanswered the converse question: "Does the historical way of thinking include the positive acknowledgment of Christianity as the highest realm of religious life and thought that has validity for us?" This question, which is of great practical importance, must now be examined.

The answer to this question, as already noted, is necessarily a matter of personal conviction. The kind of personal conviction involved here, however, is not one that derives from a dogmatic approach in which data are isolated from their historical context—that derives, in other words, from an absolutizing of Christianity that is determinative from the outset. It is a kind of personal conviction that emerges from comparative observation and absorption in hypothetically adopted values. In the former case one might well arrive at a conviction that would be materially correct and often practically satisfying, but not one that could take account of the questions and difficulties of the present intellectual situation. A conviction of the latter kind, despite the strong support it gains by its appeal to an ultimate ground, remains, however, a confession. As such, it is exposed to the attacks and ridicule of all those who refuse to recognize any truths except those capable of being demonstrated with mathematical exactness, or who regard any step beyond immediate empirical data as vague fancy or self-serving illusion. However, religious convictions that are not exposed to the opposition and mockery of the children of this world simply do not exist. Only religious platitudes enjoy this immunity. But critics like these have no monopoly on scientific reflection. It is simply that one part of reality remains hidden from their thought, while the part that is accessible looms up before them with greater integrity, distinctness, and self-sufficiency than it possesses in actuality. Consequently, a confession of the kind suggested above is thoroughly compatible with scientific perception and reflection. In matters of this kind there is no alternative but to adopt a confession based on entering into and living in accordance with the great manifestations of the spiritual life.

Despite the many difficulties of the present religious crisis, one may respond, I believe, to the question posed above with a calm and joyful affirmation of Christianity insofar as he recognizes it as the completely historical phenomenon it is. As such, Christianity combines Israelite prophecy, the preaching of Jesus, the mysticism of Paul, the idealism of Platonism and Stoicism, the integration of medieval European culture in terms of a religious conception, the Germanic individualism of Luther, and the conscientiousness and activism of Protestantism. Such a range of developments signifies both a wealth of potentialities within Christianity and a vital inner connection between Christianity and Western culture as a whole. From both we may infer not only that it is most unlikely that some new religious orientation might arise and replace Christianity, but also that it is quite possible that many new combinations will arise in the future.[1]

As far as the practical solution of religious problems is concerned, the polytheisms and polydemonisms of the lower stages of religion do not come into consideration. They are scientifically significant for the problem of the origin of religion and for that of whether religion can be traced to the human psyche. The first of these questions lies outside the scope of this inquiry and indeed cannot be answered at all. The second may here be regarded as settled in the sense that it would be misleading and wasteful to analyze these dark and turbid regions merely to show that the higher and more characteristic stages of religion cannot be derived psychologically. The higher forms of polytheism, it may be added, do have great significance for a historical understanding of what has issued from them, especially the great world religions and the philosophically reasoned critiques of religion. For the purpose of direct and genuine comparison, however, we need consider only the great world religions with their clearly supra-sensual world of absolutely transcendent religious values which enters into the world of the senses. It is these religions that free themselves from the natural confinement of religion to state, blood, and soil, and from the entanglement of divinity in the powers and phenomena of nature. It is in them that the world of the senses is solidly confronted by a higher, spiritual and eternal world, and it is in them, therefore, that the full, all-embracing power of religion first arises.

Among the world religions, the religions of law are inferior in their ability to plumb the depths of the distinction between the world of the senses and the world of higher, transcendent values. They simply juxtapose the two worlds and call for an ascent to the higher by the summoning up of powers that exist in the nature of the soul. The religions of redemption are the ones that consummate this distinction between the two worlds. They sever men inwardly from the whole of existent reality, even from the nature of their own souls, in order to confront reality with divinely empowered men. Thus they provide the whole of existent reality not only with an example of those values that overcome the world and constitute its only worth but also with the sure hope of victory and of living for a higher world.

Judaism and Islam, being offshoots of the Israelite prophetic movement, are primarily religions of law, and in neither are natural or particularistic restraints completely overcome. Among the religions of redemption, the first to be taken up is the religion that depends on the prophetic movement while essentially surpassing it, namely, the religion of Christianity. Here we find a complete and radical disengagement of God and of souls from the world; the elevation of both into the sphere of personality where nature is shaped and overcome and where unconditioned value is realized; and the overcoming of all that is merely given, merely existent, by an infinite and intrinsic value that bursts forth from the depths of the world and finds expression in practical conduct. Then comes the category of the Indian religions of redemption, similar in many respects to Neoplatonism and to the religious movements of late antiquity that coalesced in so-called Gnosticism. In the Indian religions the idea of divinity outgrows its earlier foundation in the nature religions and stifles the beginnings of personalization and ethicization that had been attained in polytheistically informed cultures. Divinity now comes to mean pure, highest being, or the supreme order of the world, in relation to which the world process signifies that this being, this order, is made obscure and finite. Redemption means, accordingly, the annulment of the world process and the obliteration of everything personal in pure being, since the existence and value of the personal constitute no problem for this type of religious apprehension.

The religions of law, Judaism and Islam, border on the redemption religions by virtue of the promises they contain. Even in the higher forms of polytheism the religious self-consciousness brings forth mystical desires and proclamations of salvation. However, redemption conceived on the basis of law remains forever bound to achievements that man produces out of his own nature, while the redeeming divinity conceived on the basis of what were originally nature religions always remains a thing-like being that lacks the vital, activating power needed to tear men away from the world and return them, transformed, to confront the world again.

Divinity of the kind found in the Indian religions has to be apprehended in self-renunciation and strenuous spiritual exercises as an impersonal, eternally existent thing, as an ultimate abstraction from the given and actual. This circumstance is decisive not only for Christianity's relationship to the concepts of redemption it first met with in Platonism and an obscure syncretism, but also and above all for its relationship to the Indian religions of redemption. These Indian religions did not go through the experience of discovering the value of personal life as the prophetic movement did. Both Brahmanic acosmism and Buddhist quietism are examples of the redemption concept as worked out by religious and ethical introspection and combined with a dialectical critique based on nature religion. In one form of development the divine turns into the Absolute One, the Eternal and Immutable. Contrasted with this Immutable One, everything in the world that is finite and transitory, together with all pain and joy, is mere illusion. By the same token, knowledge of the divine means emancipation from the world in that it blends God and the soul into one, absolutely indistinguishable unity. In a second form the divine is totally transmuted into the ordering power behind the sequence of worldly events, or into the void of bliss that lies behind the world. What leads to this blissful void is not speculation but the practical subduing of the will together with learning to know the illusoriness or nonsubstantiality of everything finite. In both forms effectual influence is exerted by ethical ideas of mastery over the self and the world, and by acute religious perceptions of the antithesis between the true and the illusory worlds. In the first form, however, the divine is a barren One, an ultimate abstraction from the existent, the only way to this One being a way of self-redemption through contemplation and asceticism. In the other it is sheer order, sheer fate, that makes self-redemption possible through the subduing of the will and the attainment of right knowledge, crowning this endeavor with participation in its own void. The juxtaposition of worlds lacks, in both cases, the truth, power, and vitality of the higher world. For this reason the higher world is here incapable of uprooting and transforming men but has to be sought out by the enlightened through appeal to self-exertion and the natural power of the soul.

Among the great religions, Christianity is in actuality the

strongest and most concentrated revelation of personalistic religious apprehension. It is even more than that. It occupies a unique position in that it alone has worked out in a radical way the distinction between the higher and lower worlds that is found on every hand. It alone, by virtue of a higher world deriving from its own reality and inner necessity, takes empirical reality as actually given and experienced, builds upon it, transforms it, and at length raises it up to a new level. It makes this achievement possible by redemptively uniting souls that are ensnared in the world and in guilt with the outgoing and embracing love of God. Christianity represents the only complete break with the limits and conditions of nature religion. It represents the only depiction of the higher world as infinitely valuable personal life that conditions and shapes all else. It renounces the world, but only to the extent that its superficial, natural significance clings to it and the evil in it has become dominant. It affirms the world to the extent that it is from God and is perceived by men of faith as deriving from and leading to God. And renunciation and affirmation, taken together, disclose the true higher world in a power and independence that are experienced nowhere else.

It is necessary to make a choice between redemption through meditation on Transcendent Being or non-Being and redemption through faithful, trusting participation in the person-like character of God, the ground of all life and of all genuine value. This is a choice that depends on religious conviction, not scientific demonstration. The higher goal and the greater profundity of life are found on the side of personalistic religion.

However difficult the problems that personalistic religion naturally raises for an empirical consideration of historical data, and however much the choice for redemption of this kind remains purely a matter of religious conviction, there are, nevertheless, certain general considerations that lift this choice above the dimension of mere arbitrariness. An approach based on the historical study of religion shows beyond doubt that Christianity not only occupies a unique position in principle but, more important, that in this unique position it also synthesizes separate tendencies and suggestions into one common goal. We gain an understanding of this goal when we examine the religions sympathetically for the purpose of determining what forces have come to expression in them, and when we speak, impelled by the imperative of inner conviction, of higher and lower stages. Just as what was explained above with regard to the matter of a norm or criterion is apposite here, so too, what was suggested above concerning the idea of evolution in the history of religions now becomes relevant.

Experience teaches that in all great religions certain basic concepts, impulses, and desires exist in interrelation. The tendencies in which the inner influence of these factors is most intensive and in which we perceive religious power working most profoundly afford us with reference points where we can see that which they have in common, that which is everywhere sought for, that which from time to time comes to forceful expression and yet remains bound to the limitations that are everywhere so difficult to exceed. Universally, the higher religious life is comprised of four sets of ideas: God, the world, the soul, and the higher life beyond this world—the world of the transcendent—that is actualized in the interrelation of the first three. These are specifically religious ideas which doubtless presuppose a certain flexibility and loftiness in a culture as a whole, but which have only an incidental relation to the concepts utilized in scientific reflection. For each of these ideas and their reciprocal relation it may now be shown that the goal toward which they strive is attained with complete independence and power in Christianity.

The concept of God, wherever it is found, contains tendencies that make for unity, sensitivity to religious values, morality, and differentiation between God and the world as well as between God and the soul. The ideas of the world and the soul, again, develop in sharp contrast to each other as well as to the idea of God. In the development of this contrast, however, there exists at the same time an awareness of a higher life, surpassing sense experience, in which such antitheses are overcome. In this sense there exists an awareness of participation in redemption. But even though these tendencies become perceptible at diverse points, and in each situation appear as bearers of profound religious power, they always remain—except in the case of Christianity—restricted and hemmed in by a narrow understanding of the original manifestation of God in the existence and works of nature. They are further held in check by the understanding of man as one who simply *is* man rather than as one who *becomes* man in self-surrender and ethical conduct. The religions of law proclaim the divine will, but they leave the natural man to overcome the world in his own strength. The non-Christian religions of redemption dissolve man and the world in the divine essence but in the process forfeit all positive meaning and content in the divine nature. Only Christianity has overcome this way of looking at things that actually represents a vestige of nature religion. Only Christianity has disclosed a living deity who is act and will in contrast to all that is merely existent, who separates the soul from the merely existent and in this separation unites it with himself. In this way the soul, purified from guilt and pride and granted assurance and security, is set to work in the world for the upbuilding of a kingdom of pure personal values, for the upbuilding of the Kingdom of God.[2]

Thus Christianity must be understood not only as the culmination point but also as the convergence point of all the developmental tendencies that can be discerned in religion. It may therefore be designated, in contrast to other religions, as the focal synthesis of all religious tendencies and the disclosure of what is in principle a new way of life. That this new life is not synonymous with the realization of a universal principle of religion established by abstraction need not be repeated. Christianity is the culmination point not despite but in terms of its particularity and distinctive features, and on this basis the goal of religion undergoes decisively new determinations.

By the same token it must not be forgotten that this revelation of the highest, purest, and most powerful religious life is a historical reality with all the individual and temporal limitations that apply to historical phenomena, and that it must retain these limitations no matter what form it takes on this earth. For this reason it cannot be proved with absolute certainty that Christianity will always remain the final culmination point, that it will never be surpassed. One may indeed find the deepest demands of human nature fulfilled in Christianity, but they are nevertheless demands which, for the most part, Christianity itself has made men aware of, and it is not impossible that a higher revelation might make men aware of even more profound postulates. However little one may speak of an actual eclipsing of Christianity to date, and however much, on the contrary, religious power of the highest consequence can be traced to it alone, convincing proof that Christianity is the final religion cannot be derived from these considerations. At this point proofs come to an end. Here there is simply the self-confident faith that absolutely nothing can make a new and higher religion likely for us. There is simply the faith that just as Christianity represented an essentially new level in contrast to all that preceded it, so all augmentation in the scale and profundity of life up to the present time has been effected on Christian premises alone. Faith may regard Christianity, therefore, as a heightening of the religious standard in terms of which the inner life of man will continue to exist. But we cannot and must not regard it as an absolute, perfect, immutable truth.

In support of this judgment we may appeal, moreover, to Christianity itself. For quite apart from the demands of historical thinking, one of the ideas intrinsic to Christianity is that while it indeed proclaims a participation in the divine life and confers the strength and certitude that accompany such participation, absolute truth belongs to the future and will appear in the judgment of God and the cessation of earthly history. Thus even on its own premises, the absolute lies beyond history and is a truth that in many respects remains veiled.

Again, if every conceivable possibility is to be taken into account, then we must also reckon with the idea that our entire Western civilization, rooted as it is in antiquity and in Christianity, might someday be thrown back into a state of barbarism. This would mean, no doubt, the end of Christianity in its present form, that is, in its relation to the person of Jesus and to its other historical foundations. But the truth and value of its personalistic understanding of redemption would not thereby be eradicated.

Anyone who recalls the hundreds of thousands of years that man has already been in existence cannot fail to conclude that personalistic redemption-religion would return in different historical forms and either reconstitute itself out of what remains of the old or fashion itself anew.

These are only outside possibilities, but they must not be permitted to drop out of sight. In order to dispel every remnant of skepticism and uncertainty, they must be kept in view. Yet even in the face of these possibilities we have no reason to think of the personalistic redemption-religion embodied in Christianity as something already disposed of or destined for destruction.

5

USEFULNESS
OF
THIS
APPROACH

Here again let us try to formulate the main conclusion reached in the preceding section of this inquiry.

The personalistic redemption-religion of Christianity is the highest and most significantly developed world of religious life that we know, being grounded in the prophets and in Jesus, possessing its primary and classical attestation in the Bible, and having disclosed a wealth of potentialities in its fusion with the culture of antiquity and with that of the Germanic tribes of western Europe. The authentic life it contains will endure in every conceivable future development. Its authentic life may be assimilated by such development, but it will never be annulled. And if it is incumbent upon us to consider the possibility of a disruption and decline of culture and of religious development, we still have every reason to believe that this authentic life will reappear and make a fresh start in a form analogous to the Christianity we know.

That is our situation, and only in this sense is it possible to affirm the "absoluteness of Christianity." This judgment issues from a joining together of absolute decision in the present with an interpretation of the developmental process that affirms historical relativity. It cannot emerge from repeated demonstrations of how Christianity, taken as an isolated object, produces an impression of absolute miracle, nor can it be deduced from the developmental process as a certain and verifiable law. In both positions something authentic has been recognized, but neither is exhaustive; instead, each must be worked out in and with the other. The "absoluteness" to which this inquiry has led us is simply the highest value discernible in history and the certainty of having found the way that leads to perfect truth.

This conclusion leads to the further question of whether an "absoluteness" of this kind can satisfy ordinary devout people in their acknowledgment of and quest for God. He who is not aware of the problem out of which this solution arises of course need not trouble himself with this question. He can cling to the old means of assurance and need not be disturbed. Again, this is not the question of whether a conviction of this kind would suffice for the creation of the great ecclesiastical organizations, or whether these institutions require a more rigorously circumscribed, bluntly intolerant and intransigent absoluteness in their concept of truth. They definitely do require this kind of absoluteness. However, the churches have, after all, now been created. The zeal and dogmatic rigidity necessary for bringing them into existence need not be continued indefinitely, since these forms that give shape to the religious life were created by periods of culture quite different from our own.

The question is, rather, whether an "absoluteness" of the kind suggested here can satisfy ordinary religious people whose modes of perception and reflection are those of the modern world, and above all whether it can serve our clergymen and theologians. These latter, by virtue of the broad, humanistic education they have received from preparatory school and university, from literature and life, have been thrust into all the problems of modern culture. The question to be considered now is whether this kind of absoluteness can provide them with a foundation from which they can derive encouragement as they carry on their work. They need certainty and joy, and deliverance from the apologetic cares that constantly threaten them anew, in order to receive the strength that frees them for their never-ending, indispensable, and glorious vocation of religious and ethical proclamation, counseling, and education. They should not preach this apologetic, but taking it as their foundation, they should be independent of each and every apologetic and free to move from person to person with the one thing that really counts: the power of simple conviction. Is that possible on this basis?

This question too may be given an affirmative answer.

The religious man wants to possess truth, genuinely desires to find God, yearns to cling to an authentic revelation and manifestation of God. For this, however, does he require an absolute religion, a knowledge of God that exhausts its essence and idea, that is withdrawn from all change and enrichment, that overleaps the bounds of history? Or if, with an admittedly quite unjustified attenuating of the word, one defines absolute religion as meaning only that pinnacle of religious knowledge which has definitely been reached and can never be surpassed, is the principal thing one needs for his own religious life the certainty that subsequent generations will never attain a higher knowledge of God? Is there not contained in such demands all too much of the natural, human presumptuousness that would vault over the boundaries and conditionality of life and transpose itself at once to the perfect goal where there is a cessation of toil, conflict, and difficulty over this matter of truth? Is not this presumptuousness unbecoming, especially in the faithful, who, because of their own spiritual struggles and their own lack of conviction and strength, ought to understand how deceptive the riddle of earthly life is better than the superficial crowd that strives self-confidently for perfect solutions? Does it not reflect mere timidity and inner uncertainty for one to become completely certain about a religious orientation whose power he has actually experienced only when he knows that it must be experienced in *this* way, in *this* historical context, and in *this* form of thought? that it must be experienced as we ourselves experience it today?

Is not the principal need of the religious man, rather, the real and innermost certainty of having encountered God and heard his voice? of following, from among the mandates of God of which he becomes aware, those that strike him as particularly plain, simple, and impelling? of committing to God the question of how He will proceed from this point on? If so, can he not be certain that what he has felt inwardly and tested in experience as the truth of life can never in all eternity become untruth? Can it be a threat to him if it is sheer faith which asserts that beyond the revelation of God in Jesus there is nothing higher to be hoped for in our entire range of vision? That assertion is, to be sure, only a statement of probability. But is this probability something we may snobbishly scorn or disdain when our knowledge is still so obscure and confused that all confidence in the existence and victory of the Spirit is itself a probability judgment only partially supported by observation and experience? when even the boldest theories of religion have attained no further than the instinctive probability judgment that God would not undertake such a display of miraculous powers and extraordinary manifestations twice or even more frequently?

With statements of this kind we have admittedly made a transition from scientific discourse to religious: from scientific substantiation by means of universal principles, laws, and necessary relations, to religious reflection upon the immediate value of a religious orientation for our life and feeling. It is the tone of the sermon or meditation that we have sounded. However, in view of the question under consideration, it can hardly be otherwise. The only kind of person who might wish to have it differently is the "scientistic" fanatic, who refuses to trust his own beliefs and values unless he has first translated them into seemingly scientific propositions, but as long as that eludes him, renounces any direct affirmation of life.

Our reflections up to this point have discharged our obligation to science; the question now is whether the outlook we have acquired in encounter with science and which we recognize as scientifically possible can suffice for the practical life of immediate perceptions and decisions, and if so, how it should be shaped to serve such a life. Consideration of this question is possible, however, only in an atmosphere of religious meditation or reflection in which appeal is made to the immediate sense of religiously and ethically involved selfhood.[1] Were this not so, the monist could not account for the adequacy of his pantheism, or the humanist for the excellence of Hellenistic education, or the prophet of the future for the preeminence of the superman. Untroubled by the reproach that we have turned to preaching, we continue, therefore, in this specifically religious mode of discourse.

The religious man needs certainty, the certainty that he is on the right path, that he is following the right star. Where differing paths to God appear before him, he will choose the one that self-involvement and conscience point out to him as most authentic, and he will seek to guide along this path all who share his understanding of what religion is, or who can be led into this understanding. However, he does not need to believe that he possesses the truth to the exclusion of everybody else any more than he needs to believe that he possesses the truth in complete and final form. It is enough if he is certain that he has the best and most profound truth that exists, and that it is useless to look beyond this truth for something higher which does not exist and which he cannot concoct himself.

Accordingly, he will be a Christian because he discerns in Christianity the purest and most forceful revelation of the higher world. He will see in the Christian faith not the absolute but the normative religion, the religion that is normative not only for him personally but also for all history up to the present time. But if he does this, he will at the same time discover that Christianity occupies a unique position which signifies an essentially new level of development. He will sense the certainty that inheres in Christianity and is bound, in Christianity more intimately than anywhere else, to the stamp of its founder's personality—the certainty, that is, of a radical and definitive revelation of God that inaugurates a new life. With this he will come to believe that he is involved with the religion that is normative not only for him and for all history up to the present but also for the future.

He will clarify and confirm this belief with a teleological and evolutionary understanding of history and will value highly the probability judgments that such an understanding makes possible, since in this sphere other kinds of judgments are withheld from men. He will not, however, make his existence as a Christian dependent on these theories. That rests on his own inner experience and its relation to the religious orientations around us. His ultimate basis of decision will always be that nowhere can he find God as he does in the prophetic and Christian world, that here he actually has found God, and that consequently, no matter what God may do with men, this faith will never deceive him.

For him, the present is summoned to rely upon Jesus, who is the source and illustration of this entire world of life, and without whose central position in our faith no religious community that perpetuates him is conceivable. The commitment of any imaginable future to Jesus is, for him, a matter that is given with and follows from faith, not a dogmatic theory that one must espouse in order to be a Christian at all.

The religious man needs the absolute, the intervention of a world of unlimited powers and ultimate values, and this means, in a word, that he needs God. Only in God, the source of all historical life, and not in a particular historical phenomenon, does he possess the absolute. He possesses this absolute in two forms: first, as the certainty that there is in reality an ultimate, infinitely valuable goal, and second, as a present knowledge of God that serves as a guarantee of the future. In the historical life-process he has access to this absolute, however, only in a historical way, a way conditioned by the context of which he is a part. It is available to him only in historically individualized revelations of the absolute that are suggestive of the future, revelations of that which transcends history and is eternally and unconditionally valuable. All he can do is to desire true participation in and true inner contact with the absolute and to seek the most forceful and profound God-centered life in the various historical manifestations where such participation is indicated. Yet at the point he finds it, he himself will be the first to admit that he has become a recipient of this life in a purely historical way, and that in terms of his own existence it is only in a historical way that it can take shape.

To wish to possess the absolute in an absolute way at a particular point in history is a delusion. It shatters not only because of its impracticability but also because it runs counter to the nature of every historical expression of religion. Wherever this delusion has crystallized into serious theories, there has swept over religion a doctrinaire rigidity and a deathlike chill that dispel the mysterious semidarkness in which alone the animating power of religion is communicated, in which man first becomes aware of his pettiness and meanness, and in which—through intuition and faith—he first senses his true dimensions. Alternatively, this delusion may result in a harsh fanaticism that loses sight of all tenderness and magnanimity and that tries to force everyone to acknowledge what the zealot possesses and understands with such certainty. That is why living piety that speaks out of its relation with God has never put forward such theories; it has called for a simple decision pro or con, but has left the matter of absolute truth to the future, to the end of history.

All that the Christian needs, therefore, is the certainty that within the Christian orientation of life there is an authentic revelation of God and that nowhere is a greater revelation to be found. This certainty he can discover even in a purely historical consideration of Christianity. In such a consideration the faith in God that animated Jesus and his followers encounters him with a power that is irresistibly transforming, profoundly moving, and binding in the highest degree. With complete composure he can consign to the world to come the absolute religion that represents not struggling faith but changeless and certain knowledge of the truth.

In justification for so doing, he will appeal above all to the preaching of Jesus himself. Wherever Jesus went, he referred in a completely unprejudiced way to the revelation of God and the knowledge of God present in those he met with, and he drew them into the challenge and promise that he, as the definitive word of the Father, proclaimed as the highest truth, the truth decisive for man's eternal destiny. To this truth every man was to hold fast in simple honesty and purity of heart and, in the power of God, thus make himself ready for the future. Only the future would bring complete deliverance, perfect knowledge, and permanent victory. What Jesus brings is simply the highest and definitive truth, the truth that is bound to endure, the truth that receives from him a power which grasps a man inwardly and totally. Yet it is this same Jesus who relegated the absolute religion to the world to come. Even the connection between the future and himself he expressed only in the form of the unhesitating confidence that the will and promise of the Father are disclosed in their fullness in what he proclaimed.

It was apologetic thinking that sought to isolate and safeguard this freely given truth. Even in the primitive church, apologetic thinking snuffed out all other lights in order to let the light of Jesus shine alone, locating the complete deliverance of the future in his passion and death in order to bind everything in an absolute way to faith in Jesus. If Jesus is the only authentic revelation, it obviously follows that he is the only normative and enduring revelation as well. If redemption is already effected in principle in what he did, then it is self-evident that the entire future remains bound to him.

The modern study of history has clearly renounced this artificial and forced isolation of a particular historical phenomenon. But even for those who follow the historical approach, Jesus remains the source of all transcendent power for living in reliance upon God and the source of all hope of victory. For this reason, as well as because of the absence of even a trace of a higher religious orientation, historical thinking confirms Christianity in its bold confidence and challenging claim that the higher religious life of mankind will continue to issue from it alone.

Just as a historical consideration of Christianity is sufficient to confirm the Christian orientation and its reliability in the realm of personal religious faith, so in the same way, a historical consideration by no means detracts from Christianity or makes it less significant as an overall phenomenon. Christianity will not turn into a superfluous relic in the history of religions, something to be treated with the utmost academic aloofness and indifference, as if its every tradition were to be doubted and torn to shreds, or as if everything unprecedented and extraordinary in Christianity were to be reduced to the level of the trivial and commonplace. Even if its history is depicted in glorified apologetic hues in the recollection of the faithful, it need not on that account be treated like a criminal whose every utterance is to be heard with the greatest mistrust and with regard to whom every suspicion is to be deemed probable from the outset.

Christianity should be studied, rather, with all the love and devotion we are bound to feel in the presence of the highest religious revelation known to mankind. The sublime miracle of its origin and development will appear none the less compelling to a perspective which sees other religions too as sublime miracles.

Adoption of the historical outlook will not brand as fictitious all that is irrational and mysterious, all the great and powerful accomplishments of the awakened spirit in its confrontation with the given, or the unusual emphasis on specifically religious personalities as we encounter them in other religions. We shall not find that all this changes into incredible fables or stamps the history of religions as the collecting of fairy tales simply because we know something about the psychology of legend. It is just the other way around. The noblest and loftiest, if also the most difficult, of tasks will continue to be that of investigating Christianity, this immensely powerful event of history, this foundation of our entire cultural life, with every method of historical research at our command. The picture of Christianity that we thus acquire, even given the uncertainty of tradition, will in its main features appear clearly before our eyes as the supreme inspiration of awe and admiration.

What we see is that above the debris of the ethnic religions of antiquity there arises, out of the tiny Jewish nation, a powerful religious orientation which attracts to itself not only all the unattached religious energies of that disrupted world but also all its new and profoundly significant religious movements. The spirit of a single man who lived entirely within the thought patterns of his people and yet possessed an incomparably creative originality, who addressed his life to what is greatest and most difficult and yet for whom the simplest was the most powerful, overflows into the lives of the nameless, of the weak and oppressed, of the unknown heroes of suffering and labor, of unphilosophical and unlettered men. Then soaring above them, the spirit of this one man renews a weary world, leavens the state, family and business, science and art with new powers, and confronts the entire future with the great problem of how to relate the changing and conditioned values of culture to the one true and abiding value of life—the value of religion.

This picture will endure as one that does in truth awaken awe and devotion, and from its points of greatest brilliance radiate animating beams of inexhaustible religious power, even though all this has taken place within the limits of historical conditionality and even though man's many failings are no less conspicuous here than elsewhere. Without being anxious about these matters, the religious man may go on seeing in Christianity the history of his salvation and receiving from it the edifying, strengthening, and integrating power that is forfeited by anyone who tries to produce out of his mind alone a religion that hangs suspended in the unconditioned vacuum of rational necessity.

Christianity remains *the* great revelation of God to men, though the other religions, with all the power they possess for lifting men above guilt, grief, and earthly life, are likewise revelations of God, and though no theory can rule out the abstract possibility of further revelations. Christianity remains *the* deliverance, even though the power over the natural man and his cravings which is at work in every religion is also genuine deliverance, and even though Christianity's deliverance takes a step forward in history whenever faith in God is planted in weak and sinful hearts. Above all, Christianity remains the work of Jesus, having its greatest strength in its relationship to him and drawing its confidence from the authentic and living guarantee of the grace of God in his personality. Even though we discern the power and activity of God in other heroes and prophets of religion, it is in Christianity, more profoundly than anywhere else, that faith in God is bound up with the vision of the life and passion of him who reveals and guarantees that faith. Even though we cannot disprove the possibility that Jesus might someday be surpassed, the fact remains that we are all too weak to detect any higher power of God in our hearts. Instead, we gain peace and joy only through submission to him and his Kingdom. We are left, therefore, with the Christian community of life and spirit as the only fellowship of faith and love that proceeds from him and that in proclaiming him is nourished and sustained.

This community needs no other foundation than the certainty that in him it has access to the highest religious and ethical power. It needs no apologetic that would make this truth truer by depriving everything outside Christianity of godly life and power in order to confer them in some absolute or supernatural way upon Christianity.

The religious man loses nothing of this kind by a plain and simple historical approach to Christianity. On the contrary, by such an approach he is set free from all kinds of cares and problems whose artificial solutions never did lead to genuine peace but only plunged him into ever new artificialities. He need not be alarmed if he discovers elements related to Christianity in Buddhism or Zoroastrianism; if he finds in Plato, Epictetus, or Plotinus religious ideas and powers that are actually or apparently parallels and anticipations of Christianity. God is alive and manifest in them, too, and it is clearly evident that their religious powers have flowed into the Christian belief in God and into the Christian idea of personality and greatly augmented their growth. The religious man need not shrink back if he finds Christianity living on earlier religious developments that form part of its present environment, or if Asiatic syncretism, like the Hellenic ethic and philosophy of religion, converges with and flows into the Christian religion. These too are all, in their own right, living religious movements in which God is at work, and Christianity has been nourished by all these elements that it encounters and to which it is related. Indeed, it has become Christianity's distinctive task to make itself the crystallization point for the highest and best that has been discovered in the human spiritual world, its fitness for this task of attracting and sustaining such values being due to its superior power.

Above all, one need not take fright if he sees that Jesus himself, together with his first apostles, was greatly influenced by ideas that were current in Judaism and in antiquity generally but are utterly alien to us today. These ideas themselves proceeded from living religious apprehension; primitive Christians lived in terms of these ideas, accepting them as a self-evident frame of reference that constituted the presupposition of the new religious stirrings. These people were men of the ancient past, Jews, men of the people. If here, as elsewhere, religious renewal issued from the common people and not from the heights of refined and skeptical sophistication, it is also self-evident that the horizon of the people was not limited to religious concepts alone. The new religious orientation took shape out of the world view and basic ideas of what till that time had been Jewish folk religion. For this reason, however, the new religious orientation was as yet free of preoccupation with philosophy and theology, of conceptual artifices that waste the living substance of the will, and of disputatiousness over the letter of the law. The criticisms it involved were purely ethical and religious in nature. As a result, the new religious idea retained an unspeculative purity and greatness that made possible its separation from its initial Jewish forms.

Finally, one should not be surprised by the knowledge that this separation from Judaism simply led to the substitution of new limitations as elements of Greek religion coalesced with Christianity, or by the knowledge that the religious idea and its power alike swiftly subsided from their original eminence and poured out onto the lowlands of the commonplace. But what was commonplace in primitive Christianity still represented an elevation of the inner life, and from it flowed power to fashion new disclosures in which we, though always in a historically conditioned way, experience the liberating greatness of the Christian idea up to the present day.

The knowledge we have gained of the necessary relativity of every moment of historical existence cannot devalue the period in which Christianity was born, or the present moment, or that which lies between. Our ethical and religious judgment enables us to weigh the significance of these periods in relation to each other, just as it enables us to assess the value of Christianity in relation to other religions. In all this we know ourselves to be on the road that leads to the goal of history, the occasion and nature of which we leave to God. We are on the course and in the movement of life that leads to the absolute when we dedicate ourselves to the living world of personalistic religion and perceive in Christianity its embodiment in our cultural context and our moment of history. All other religious orientations take their place beside or behind us as ideas that have not yet achieved the breakthrough to personalism. This is enough to provide us with that sense of the absolute which we need and which we can attain.

6
TWO
TYPES
OF
ABSOLUTENESS

Christianity is the pinnacle of all religious development thus far and the basis and presupposition for every distinct and meaningful development in man's religious life in the future. There is no probability that it will ever be surpassed or cut off from its historical foundations as far as our historical vision can reach. That is the result we have arrived at so far in this approach which has taken historical relativity into account and has also been shown to satisfy the religious need for certainty of communion with God and for assurance of salvation.

It might appear that with this simple but significant result, everything had been accomplished. There remain, however, some final considerations that take us to the very heart of the problem. They have to do with the ultimate grounds for having misgivings about the solution suggested here and the ultimate grounds for finding it objectionable.

There is no denying the fact that the view advanced in this inquiry not only runs counter to both orthodox and liberal theology but also stands in opposition to the ecclesiastical self-understanding of Christianity worked out for the most part since the establishment of the first Christian congregations and the victory of Pauline theology. With this way of thinking do we still find ourselves within the bounds of Christianity? Can such a way of thinking have any positive significance for Christianity at all if it turns Christianity's ecclesiastical theory of absoluteness into a special instance of a self-understanding common to all religions? Does not our assessment of Christianity cut across the grain of Christianity's deep-seated tendency toward unique and exclusive truth? Conversely, does not this tendency, if really acknowledged, fall under suspicion as illusory due to its resemblance to analogous tendencies in the other world religions?

To put it differently: If a plain and simple idea of the supreme value of Christianity in the sense described above takes the place of "absoluteness," can this idea of supreme value forego a mooring in a special theory of value—a theory similar to the ecclesiastical doctrine of miracle that will make it absolutely unique and necessary—without eroding the true, inmost nature of the faith as it has till now existed? Or, conversely: Can the Christian faith really permit itself to embrace historical thinking without nullifying its many universal values?

Answering these questions leads to the very heart of the problem, namely, whether Christianity can be disengaged from the ecclesiastical form it has taken in the course of history. In taking up this question we return again to the scientific inquiry proper and to the scientific mode of discourse.[1]

This is an all-embracing question, applying not only to religion but to every kind of value that derives from the inner life, indeed, to the simplest judgments of everyday life as well. The simplest observational judgments, the most natural impulses of the will, the rules and customs traditionally passed down—all these are taken by the *naïve* man as absolute. The various expressions of the inner life of man in government, law, and business, in art, morality, and learning present themselves as absolute in their origins, their spontaneous growth, and their dominance over convention. Every form of religious devotion, within the boundaries of its sphere of influence, quite naturally and as a matter of course regards itself as absolute, and every world religion does the same in every conceivable sphere. Absoluteness is a universal characteristic of the naïve way of thinking.

Equally universal, however, is the process that leads to the limitation or dissolution of such naïve conviction. Comparison between religions and the realization that one has to make adjustments in his initial, naïve outlook has a shattering effect on absoluteness and paves the way for *thinking*. Freedom from this first naïve absoluteness is the essence of culture, and attaining it invariably results in all kinds of struggles and camouflages due to the feeling that this separation will involve the loss of some original vitality.

In order to secure a basis for correcting this initial, spontaneous outlook and for directing it with greater certainty, one seeks for constant relationships. One seeks for a universal by which to comprehend the particular aright and locate it in its context. From the first crude and simple corrections in the way things initially appear to the senses, an unbroken chain of analyses, comparisons, new syntheses and combinations leads to a reinterpretation of reality—superficial in some ways, profound in others—in which absoluteness is attributed to no single particular but only to the most comprehensive integrating principles.

The same holds true in the case of intellectual values and religions. Thwarted expectations, disillusioning comparisons between what religion says about how things should be understood as over against ways of understanding that originate in other quarters, the clash and contradiction of ideas, and especially the opposition between different kinds of religion: all this leads to comparisons and adjustments that result in a transformation of the initial naïve position. This process continues until all the different kinds of religion have been juxtaposed, until all the contradictions and antitheses have been matched point for point in an effort to discover in these correlations an ultimate principle that will make possible a unified and coherent account and assessment of the whole.

In this way *the naïve world view changes into a scientific one.* The latter, in ever widening circles, makes direct observation and appraisal by correlation and synthesis into a problem for scientific inquiry, and with mounting urgency it seeks either to re-establish universal and necessary concepts that are abstracted from transient forms of being in the course of such inquiry, or to delimit them or even set them aside in favor of better, truer, and more reliable concepts. This transformation of the naïve world view into the scientific one has made the earth revolve around the sun and the sun around invisible galaxies. It has made knowledge adapt itself not merely to things but to the laws and exigencies of the mind. It has transformed objective cultural values into paradoxically rich human achievements. Moreover, it has compelled the self-certainty that spontaneously attaches itself to religion to take note of scientific arguments and discussions in which in the last analysis religion, psychologically considered, is taken as a highly conditioned phenomenon of the human subject and, historically considered, as a limitless realm of individual religions that for the most part advance similar claims.

Thus the problem before us is, to put it concisely, *the general problem of the relationship of the naïve world view to the scientific in its application to religion.* The pain, doubt, anxiety, and uncertainty that science engenders when applied to religion are no different from the tensions that have been and are occasioned wherever a scientific understanding of the world intrudes upon men who have their roots in naïve, conventional modes of thought and value judgment. Similarly, the ways of resolving these tensions are no different in the religious sphere from those by which science everywhere tries to take particulars that exist as isolated fragments and reestablish them in some kind of reconstruction on the basis of a known overall context. Just as in other spheres, so in relation to religion the scientific way of thinking cannot be used without having a profoundly transforming effect. Accordingly, the cleverness that so many theologians are in quest of, cleverness akin to that of squaring the circle or washing an animal skin without getting it wet, is no more attainable here than anywhere else. The agitation and pain that everywhere attend the transition from naïve to scientific thinking are to be avoided least of all in the realm of religion.

On the other hand, what is true of scientific thought everywhere else is true of it in the area of religion as well: It transforms one's initial understanding, but it does not thereby invalidate the objective reality to which this immediate understanding refers. It merely gives it a changed conception and frame of reference. The absoluteness of which one is convinced simply shifts from the particular understood in isolation, to the context on the basis of which the particular is now to be understood.

Just as the most radical and thoroughgoing skeptic preserves a residuum of the reality on which naïve thought relies in his affirmation of the necessity of skepticism, so too the most radical denier of religion retains a remnant of the reality on which naïve religion depends in his attempts to explain the religious phenomenon. But where excesses have been avoided in the transformation of the naïve outlook, the goal of science, rightly understood, is to reinstate naïvely perceived reality at a higher level within the framework of as comprehensive a unifying context as possible.

All radicalism of thought consists, first, in recognizing that insight into the distinction between naïve and scientific ways of thinking may delude us into the false assumption that there can be a total contradiction between the true reality of scientific thought and the seeming reality of naïve apprehension, and second, in taking the general conceptions obtained from one part of reality and applying them with abstract consistency to the whole. Again, mature wisdom of thought signifies that reality as naïvely perceived is not denied but viewed in a higher context, and that the different orders and dimensions of naïvely understood reality are permitted to remain as they are if, despite the attempt to see them in context, they resist all synthesizing efforts and thus prove themselves incapable of being united. These principles are basic to epistemology.

Now if this is the way things turn out, it is clear that the scientific transformation is attended not only by pain, anxiety, and disruption but by an elevating and liberating effect as well. It releases men from the narrowness, pettiness, and intolerance of the first way of understanding and from its uncertainty, vagueness, and one-sidedness. It frees them for a dispassionate and comprehensive perspective, for generosity and gentleness of outlook, for tolerance and forbearance, and for firmness and clarity of conviction. In place of the vehement fanaticism that sees every challenge to exclusive validity as meaning that if exclusive validity goes, everything else will immediately reel and collapse, there emerges the calm certainty that true and authentic powers of reality maintain themselves even within this broader framework and that only those that were accidentally or artificially thrust into the foreground are lost or reduced to modest dimensions.

The scientific transformation produces all these effects, therefore, in the area of religion as well. What it brings upon men by way of doubt, anxiety, struggle, and pain, it makes up for by the peace and certainty of discernment that penetrates to what is essential, by tolerance and forbearance for all transient and individual forms, by generosity and comprehensiveness of perspective, and by providing men with a broader foundation for their life and thought. In this endeavor religion admittedly occupies a special position inasmuch as it constitutes the nucleus and stay for all the higher human values and thus by nature feels the unavoidable shocks of this transformation with greater pain and agitation than they are perceived anywhere else. For the same reason, however, a scientifically informed restoration of the naïve outlook, now raised to a higher level, is to the same degree more beneficial and significant for life as a whole. It frees men from the know-it-all attitudes and resultant conflicts that, among ordinary men everywhere, arise from the uncontrolled naïve outlook and that have led to fearsome terrors and vicious pettiness in the sphere of religion. Once disciplined, faith aspires again to the pure power of naïve conviction from which alone what is great and noble proceeds.

To be sure, in all highly developed cultures the will to form naïve, absolute judgments has been broken and "sicklied o'er with the pale cast of thought," but in the process life has become richer, finer, and more just. Bringing the great ecclesiastical organizations into being, for example, required a ruthless zeal on the part of men who believed that they were in possession of the one and only salvation and were obligated to realize it even by force. But in the forms that have thus been brought into being, a gentler, freer, and fairer spirit can dwell, a spirit that is capable of relative judgments and that in making them acquires a gentleness and compassion impossible in a rigid know-it-all stand.

The significance that this distinction between the naïve and the scientific orientations has for religion must therefore be considered in this concluding section. Particular attention will be given to the effect that scientific correlation and comparison have on the claims which the religions make to absoluteness.[2]

Absoluteness in the simplest and plainest sense of the word—and thus without any such connotations as would involve an antithesis with the relative or the prospect of an alleged means for overcoming this antithesis—is a universal characteristic of all naïve life. Every perception is at the moment absolute. Every determination and affirmation of value, whether of a lower or higher kind, is in the moment of its origin absolute, that is, unconditionally and unrestrictedly valid, in and of itself authoritative. Self-deception, contradictory experiences, confrontations with other outlooks and value orientations bring this absoluteness, little by little, to a point where it begins to totter. Every individual personality with its natural desires, inclinations, and habits perceives itself at first as absolute, that is, as the norm and criterion for everything else. Education, the give-and-take of controversy, ethical self-discipline, and a broadened range of experience gradually place restrictions on this absoluteness. Every society—with its traditions, customs, life relationships and patterns of association—is initially regarded as absolute, that is, as though it could not and should not be otherwise. The needs arising out of these circumstances, a growing acquaintance with other situations, and the adopting of a historical orientation bring about a breakdown in this natural self-understanding. Nevertheless, despite all these restrictions, there remains one fundamental perception on the basis of which it should be possible to restore harmony: the spontaneous presupposition of a homogeneity and solidarity in the inner, creative life of all mankind. This presupposition constitutes the basic and axiomatic idea behind the comparative and relational way of thinking stimulated by such experiences, a way of thinking that must ultimately encounter its presupposition and on that basis acquire a new orientation.

In even greater measure is this the case with all the higher cultural values. They make their appearance not only with the obviousness of that which is unquestionably real but also with the inevitableness of that which is unquestionably valid. All art, government, and social order, all mores, and especially all religion possess in their youth a sure and staunch belief in their inner necessity and undeniable validity, and this belief requires no external substantiation. In all these components of culture man possesses the necessary, the normative, the higher life that realizes intrinsically objective values. No religion can arise out of scholarship or reflection without bearing in itself the Hippocratic bias toward skepticism and the feebleness of the merely possible. Living and genuine religion, on the other hand, has always arisen out of inner necessity and because of immediate divine constraint and vocation without depending on apologetics or proofs. Purely on its own authority it has opened up a realm of higher life. All religions are born absolute, for without reflecting on the matter they simply obey a divine compulsion and proclaim a reality that demands acknowledgment and belief, not merely because of its actuality but more because of its validity. Moreover, every person of genuine and childlike faith feels the same about the beginnings and high points of his religion as people did in the period of its origin. To him too its absoluteness is a matter of course, since it involves him in a self-determining reality through which he has access to the sphere of the absolutely necessary and the absolutely valuable. Without even thinking about possible alternative forms of faith, he simply lives in terms of the dictates of absoluteness and therewith in terms of the only real truth.

Now is this *naïve absoluteness* an absurdity? Is it an illusion that must fade away as horizons expand, as differing cultural values and contending religions with similar claims present themselves side by side, and as men affirming ethical and religious values come face to face with the shattering awareness of nature's indifference to ideal values and of the weakness of ideals in the face of human mediocrity?

Naïve absoluteness in the religious realm is no more absurd than the natural absoluteness of naïve perception or spontaneous desire. Just as a theory that traces all the conditions and possibilities of seeing does not make seeing into non-seeing, so in the same way consideration and comparison of the types and presuppositions of the claims that religious faith makes to absolute values, divinely ordained principles of social order, and grounds of reality does not make these claims into their opposite. It does not reduce them to the arrogant fantasy of inordinate self-regard or the shortsighted vanity of a disputatious know-it-all outlook.

In this naïve absoluteness there exists and is communicated to the human spirit a real stimulus from the object. There further exists an ineradicable recognition of a higher life of necessary and universal validity. These inhere in naïve absoluteness in exactly the same way that every man receives stimuli from external objects and has an undeniable, natural certainty that all human perceptions are essentially homogeneous. All this is no mere delusion. It simply appears in a new context and with changed meaning as a result of enlarged perspectives. Comparison can show only the special form and conditionality of religious claims. Every such claim expresses, however, the stimulus of an objective world of the spirit and the power of values that call for realization in the ways possible in human history and therefore in unique and individual forms. This certainty is a component that accompanies whatever is objective. It maintains itself to the same degree and in the same manner that the object is, from time to time, perceived in the fullness of its power. Only when the object itself vanishes does this certainty vanish, but the object itself, for its part, redoubles its weight and strength in these conflicts with the requirements of earthly particularity. Faced with these conflicts, a man with his ardent will to live tends to withdraw from these complexities in favor of a single, compelling manifestation of life by which his will can strengthen itself once again in the power of the absolute.

Just as new religious movements are sustained in their formative periods by this sense of naïve absoluteness, so too all religious reactions to skepticism and atheism are primarily passionate eruptions of this feeling for the absolute that is so deeply rooted in men. This is where we must look for the sources of religious creativity and of all fresh, unrestrainable power. However much these various forms of natural absoluteness may require delimitation because of the complete naïveness they originally entail, there yet remains in them an element of truth, just as in natural, naïve perception. The more significant the substantive content of the original naïve absoluteness, the more firmly this reality maintains itself when relativized, and all the more easily does the will that is weary of relativities turn to it again.[3]

But if the natural absoluteness of the religions is simply the naïve component of that which is apprehended in them as real and valuable, then the form and manner in which this natural absoluteness comes to expression will differ in accordance with the manner and degree in which the higher world manifests itself in a given religion. Because this absoluteness is only a naïve reflection of that which is apprehended as real, it will differ from the real that is perceived from time to time. And if the real manifests itself in various degrees of depth and clarity, the different forms of natural absoluteness will, accordingly, differ from one another.

Alternatively, if we discover, in a religious movement that has lost its momentum, that natural absoluteness has been replaced by theories and proofs of exclusive validity, we may venture to say that here the inner dictates of absoluteness are no longer fully sensed and that it is for this reason that a forced and artificial substitute is sought. To put it succinctly, in this religious movement the true, inner constraint of absoluteness is no longer fully effective. Claims to absoluteness will thus differ greatly both in form and content. Only to a point of view that relies solely on externals will they seem to resemble each other completely. Such differences, as a matter of fact, quite plainly do exist, and they expose a gross lack of understanding on the part of those who hold that the only feature common to these claims is a want of culture and education in certain periods and among certain peoples.

Wherever found, whether in the small, polydemonistic, ethnic, and tribal religions or the great polytheisms of the civilized peoples of antiquity, natural absoluteness is inherently limited and conditioned. It reflects the nature of the divinities that hold sway over these clans, tribes, and peoples. A deity's activity, like its presence, is limited to blood and domain, to the soil of the homeland and to the precincts of sacred temples. This absoluteness holds good only for those who are bound together by ethnic ties and kinship, for those who dwell within the deity's sphere of influence. Outside that sphere, other gods may reign and be considered as equally absolute in their domains. But a great, unknown, heavenly providence overarches and at the same time works within these domains, exhibiting nature and the given world as the ground and medium of the changes it effects and the creativity it manifests. Only when we come to the great ethical and mystical world religions do we find faiths that lay claim to an unlimited absoluteness which holds good for all times and places, proclaiming variously the Creator and Lord of the world, or the order and predetermined sequence that underlie all existence, or a ground of things that upholds and nurtures the whole. To these cosmic orders they add universal imperatives that govern the human soul, a law that rules the spirit. For this reason the world religions trace their origin not to theophanies or oracular sites, and not to hoary traditions or priestly lore, but to the living certainty known by a heart that has been grasped by the power of truth. The world religions are prophetic religions and regard their founders as absolute authorities, regardless of whether they intend to win a small or a large number to this exclusive truth. But the differences do not stop here. They only become more refined and profound.

The ecstatic mysticisms and theological pantheisms that arise at various places are breakthroughs to the one thing that is essential to religion generally: the integrity of the divine and the integrity of the human. The outcome of these breakthroughs is the destruction of the naïve absoluteness of ethnic religions and a partial critique of their structures, anthropomorphisms, and myths. But with regard to the foundation from which they derive their certainty and absoluteness, these breakthroughs yield only an obscure, elusive, many-faceted idea of the Divine One that man discovers by thought and meditation or occasionally by ascetically-acquired enlightenment. Absoluteness here depends not upon an invading, apprehending will of the divine but upon the thought and action of man, who is in any case bound to act and think. As a result, the significance and the authority of the first enlightening thinker and spiritual leader are bound to ebb away. Absoluteness depends on a psychological foundation that is supposed to give rise to the same insights everywhere among all who are capable of religious knowledge. In consequence, however, absoluteness is also bound to the contingencies of the human, that is, to the capacity for and training in deeper, theological thinking, or to the unpredictable occurrence of ecstasy.

It is true that wherever movements of this kind have led to the formation of great religious communities, outstanding personalities stand in the foreground, but even here these characteristics of the absoluteness to which they lay claim continue to be clearly perceptible. Brahmanism remains the religion of a theological school and a priestly caste. The pantheisms of the Oriental religions are essentially the wisdom of priests. Buddhism is a kind of monastic order in which each of the enlightened may arrive independently at the same wisdom that the Buddha discovered. Its very existence depends on the masses of the unenlightened, insofar as it has not reconstituted itself as some form of polytheism or turned into a half-theistic redemption-religion. The syncretisms that arose toward the end of the era of the great Hellenistic religions were esoteric doctrines or ecstatically sustained products of reflection. Neoplatonism entrusted itself not to the will and power of its remote and impredicable deity but to the necessity and universal validity of its thought, by which it was borne upward through the various stages of the divine to the hope of a finite ecstasy that enabled it to attain its goal.

In these cases naïve absoluteness is limited to the obscure foundation of religious feeling, everything else being human will and artifice. But on this static, given foundation, which is the ultimate basis of the natural religious consciousness, no orientation arises which possesses the power to apprehend and mold the world as a whole or to achieve unity in the goal of the One. That happens only where God, as ethical will, stands over against nature and unites men in an ethical goal expressive of their own inner nature. Then there comes into existence a naïve absoluteness of the ethically necessary and a universal commitment to the divine revelation that manifests its goals once and for all in prophetic souls. Yet even in this case significant distinctions exist.

The prophetic religion of Zoroaster, with its fundamental conception of a battle between good and evil and its eschatological hope regarding the conclusion of this battle, undoubtedly signifies a powerful religious breakthrough to an ethical universalism that exercised considerable influence during the early stages in the development of concepts important to the gospel. However, its deity has not absorbed all lesser gods into the unity of the ethical will and even has to share the world with the principle of evil. Furthermore, its ethic binds purely moral precepts to materializing cults and ceremonies, to legal regulations and customs of a merely local kind. Therefore, the principle of a universally valid good that brings forth and governs all things is not carried to its conclusion. Instead, law and the proclamation of salvation are from the outset restricted to those who have not been irrevocably consigned to the evil spirit. Among such people, it is the Persian who, as a matter of course, is actually the chosen companion and helper of the good God. For this reason all its conceptions are intimately tied up with the scenes and images of Persian mountains and steppes, and the orientation as a whole remains, in fact, a national religion.

Even more radically, the prophetic religion of Israel differentiated between Yahweh, who arbitrarily elects and destroys, and the Hebrew people, who were perishing in the disorders of the Near East. It exalted him as ethical will over the entire world process as well as over the heathen gods. At the same time it brought into being an individual religious orientation that permitted each person, in his inner life, to be independent of the world. In the last analysis, however, this Yahweh who arbitrarily concluded the covenant and could speak with hostility even to his elect, is fettered to a renewed remnant of the covenant people. Since the religion of Israel fails to free men effectually from the bonds of blood and cultus, it has not allowed ethical universalism to share fully in the sure foundation it has in the divine nature. It has even bound this universalism in an external way to the concept of a Judaism that grows in size and grandeur. Thus the magnificent ethical gospel of the prophets has been altered into a particularistic, ritual law that acts as a serious obstacle to any form of universal validity oriented solely to the inner man.

The universalism of Islam, which has its most significant point of departure in the religious and ethical ideas of Judaism, is restricted in a different but equally severe way. From Judaism it took over monotheism and the basic features of its ethic, and in doing so it inherited a portion of inwardly oriented absoluteness, manifested in a genuinely prophetic way in the first public statements of Muhammad. However, its deity has retained too much of a dark, fatalistic arbitrariness to have any inner relation either to its own precepts or to the souls of men. In addition its precepts have incorporated too much fortuitous Arabic law and custom, together with personal spur-of-the-moment ideas of the Prophet, to permit the rise of a universalism that is really inward and necessary. Then too, when his first ardor dimmed (as was rather typical of him), Muhammad took to artificial substitutes and deliberately embodied in his work an idea that was of only secondary importance to Jews and Christians. That is the idea of a sacred book of law, whereby he has forever bound his followers to an often magnificent, but equally often inadequate and confused writing that immortalizes all kinds of Arabic idiosyncrasies.

The preaching of Jesus, however, presents a purely inward absoluteness which, together with the inwardness and genuine humanity of the religious life he exemplified, is significantly different from all the forms of ethical absoluteness referred to above. Here the universality of demand and promise are much more intimately bound up with the personal character of the Master himself, who simply proclaimed the holy and gracious will of God that is experienced in the individual soul as unconditionally valid. Yet he attributed to this message only such intrinsic authenticity and necessity as Jonah's call to repentance had! And in how pure and spontaneous a way this absoluteness and universality express the heart of the matter, the essence of the ethical will of God, acknowledging without prejudice all truth that was made known to men of old, that existed from the beginning, and that any lowly Samaritan or publican could find in his heart!

With no polemic other than that against false understanding and abuse of the divine will in human presumption and narrowness of heart, with no proof other than the certainty of his vocation and the assent of the righteous, with a conscience that did not rely on appearances or on the world, and with no side-glances at other doctrines or theologies, Jesus simply proclaimed, on the basis of the reality itself, the one thing that was needful and that was now to be made known in its full urgency to his many servants and apostles. To be sure, all his preaching has a Jewish tinge and moves within the conceptual world of popular Judaism; but what everything depends on is God—who will fulfill his promise and bring in the higher world of true life—and the soul, which is of greater worth than all the honors and delights of this world and finds its true and enduring treasure only in that higher world of the Kingdom of God.

Only in the complete individualization and humanization of religion—as was the case in Jesus' own faith and experience and in his challenge to the soul—and in the radical separation of the higher, eternal, and necessary world from the earthly and transitory, does there exist the absoluteness which the church transformed into definite faith-propositions but which, for Jesus, was simply included in the reality itself. Whatever role messianism may have played in his preaching, by and large the person of Christ retired behind this reality—the Kingdom of God.

In his preaching the Kingdom is the absolute. It proves itself to be so by the appeal it makes to the purest and inmost desires of the soul and also by the certainty of its imminent, miraculous realization by the Father, whose purposes for the world will thereby be fulfilled. Accordingly, it is taken for granted that there will be no higher revelations of the Father. Instead, everything converges on the matter of present decision in the great world struggle.

This simply confirms the result that was reached earlier. Just as Christianity develops the personalistic religious idea and its liberating power to its maximum clarity and strength, so too its natural, spontaneous absoluteness is the purest and most inwardly oriented expression of the power of religion. But if Christianity provides us with the freest and most inwardly oriented form of the idea of absoluteness among those known to us, this is simply a reflection of the substantive relationship between the Christian religion and the other major forms of religion. The various kinds of naïve absoluteness are not theories about a uniquely grounded and legitimized truth; they are expressions of the religious idea itself. The very absence of any secondary apologetic ideas shows that they regard themselves as final and conclusive truth. This does not mean, however, that they cancel each other out. Instead, their contradictions and conflicts merely reflect the principle that underlies them, the universal principle of a world of ultimate, absolute values which none of these naïve forms of religion can exhaust but can only prepare the way for, each believing—as in its isolated self-understanding it must—that in its own way it has uniquely and conclusively done so. That is why crude and superficial comparison finds in these contradictions only out-and-out antithesis. But the moment scientific thought penetrates more deeply and seeks out the point of interconnection below the surface of the phenomena, these contradictions present themselves as expressions of a common principle that guarantees the relative authenticity of them all, taking away only the initial, naïve conviction of finality and absolute uniqueness.

Since this principle makes it possible to sort and classify the various claims, it also makes it possible to arrange them in a graded series. The highest religion is the one that has the freest and most inwardly oriented claim to absoluteness, and it will stand by this claim as long as no trace of higher religious life appears anywhere else. Indeed, this claim, in all its individual historical forms, will be deemed even more enduring and unsurpassable the more Christianity proves itself to be both the convergence point of all developmental tendencies in religion and the elevation of the goal of religion to an essentially new level. A scientific approach merely involves trimming away the limitations of this claim till a point is reached where uniqueness will be understood in broader perspective as a particular aspect of a whole, and where antithesis that was first perceived atomistically will be regarded not as mutually exclusive contradiction but as antithesis between levels. To think in a scientific way about this problem means that the first, individual, historical form of Christianity must be perceived not as final but as the point of departure for constantly new historical and individual forms. It also means that during times when scientific habits of thought are exercising influence in every dimension of life, insight into the purely naïve character of claims to absoluteness is required, together with the recognition that these claims do in fact mirror the power of an objective reality.

In all this a scientific approach shows that the genuine, naïvely understood absolute is not a revelation or a historical phenomenon. It is none other than God himself in his incalculable richness of life, constantly surprising human smallness of faith with new revelations. To put it differently, the absolute is the goal of the human spirit, characterized by a boundlessness and otherworldliness that transcend all history. Wherever God or the goal of the spiritual life is strongly and vividly present to the soul, the absoluteness of God leads to religious experiences, attestations, and beliefs in a completely spontaneous way. This is as true of the great and lofty forms of religion as it is of the petty and confused forms. In their own ways they all understand themselves as absolute, and they may continue to regard themselves in this way as long as their naïve self-confidence does not ebb away. The study of history may dissolve this naïve conviction, but it always moves toward a broader context of human development that underlies all forms of religion. In terms of this frame of reference it restores a due measure of the authenticity of these naïve claims. The naïve absoluteness of the historically evolved religions is, therefore, simply the deep, inner relationship between the bearers of revelation and the God who speaks in them; and the legitimacy of these naïve claims to absoluteness may be measured by the liberating and redeeming power that issues from faith. The naïve absoluteness of Jesus is simply his faith that he had been sent by the Heavenly Father and his certainty that just as the will of the Father is the only truth by which human behavior should be governed, so the promise of the Father is the only salvation. The justification for his claim is that it flows from the purest and most powerful religious idea in a way that encounters the inner man most deeply and compellingly. The actuality involved, however, in thus connecting human life with a belief in the certainty of God is, like all immediate experience, an ultimate, irreducible element of reality, a mystery like the mystery of everything real.

Now should not faith be satisfied with this naïve claim of the gospel, the purest and strongest of the religious claims, on the ground that it is the expression of the purest and strongest religious power?

It would be easier to answer this question if the whole of our religious understanding were not profoundly influenced by ecclesiastical theology and apologetics, which in turn have their roots in the faith and theology of the primitive Christian fellowship. For the earliest Christian fellowship, at any rate, as well as for the subsequently elaborated church, this absoluteness did not suffice, and the New Testament is full of attempts to buttress this naïve certainty with apologetic reflections. Indeed the distinctive difference between the preaching of Jesus and its early portrayal in the faith of primitive Christianity is that Jesus, with his free and unrestrained spontaneity, saw absoluteness in the reality itself, in the Kingdom of God. On the other hand, when the early Christians gathered to revere Jesus as Messiah, Atoner, and Heavenly Master, they transferred this absoluteness to the person of the Messiah and Lord. Accordingly, his person became absolutized, and the significance now attached to the person of the Redeemer had to be supported by all kinds of scriptural proofs and Gnostic speculations.

It is not as if developed theories or doubts based on principle were here being contested, nor as if the embryonic church had already brought forth a theology of its own. Instead, a number of motives and circumstances converged: the natural distance between the believing congregation and its Lord and Master, leading to the greatest conceivable exaltation and isolation of the Master; the natural dogmatism of a childlike way of thinking that tends to dissolve relationships and see things in isolation;

the credulous admiration that carries everything before it and aspires to infinity; the need of the early Christian fellowship to have a stable and consistent foundation of its own; the development of this fellowship into a new religion based on the worship of Christ, baptism, and the Lord's Supper; and finally, the struggle that soon arose with Judaism as well as with syncretism. All these things, even in the earliest period, permitted the naïve claim of Jesus to be subordinated to theories that were supposed to provide it with a foundation. Indeed without such a foundation, the growing fellowship could hardly fashion a durable center for itself.

The Messiah-faith of the primitive fellowship and the Christ-mysticism of Paul represent what is as yet the naïve beginning of dogmatic thought, the embryo of ecclesiastical dogma and apologetics. Only after it ascended into the cultivated, literary world and encountered scholarship and philosophical religion was this theory brought to completion, finding its definitive form in the doctrines of the Trinity and of original sin. Even miracle, caught up into this development, outgrew the dimension of what was immediately obvious and was transposed into that of theological theory.

Thus out of naïve absoluteness an *artificial, apologetic absoluteness* arose. The certainty of the divine challenge and promise gave way to the lifting up of miraculous events and relations as the foundation for a theological theory of the uniqueness of Christianity. Artificial absoluteness sprang up not because of error or arbitrariness but under the pressure of circumstances, modeling itself on the prototype provided by Jewish theology and on the patterns of speculation developed by the syncretistic religions of reform. Above all, it came into being because of a lack of historical or critical understanding. Indeed that entire era was bereft of any such understanding, though that was the one thing that could have impeded the development of such an apologetic. During a history of nearly two thousand years, this apologetic has woven itself so deeply into our sense of what it means to be Christian that we now seem dependent on artificial absoluteness. It now seems essential to hold to a theory in which Christianity will differ completely from everything else in history because of the miraculous causation of its origin and the miraculous power that attests its validity and, by virtue of this unique position, be the only religion capable of providing a permanent basis for salvation.

But in the modern world doctrine embellished by this kind of apologetic clashes sharply and irrevocably not only with the enormous transformation that has taken place in our understanding of things generally, but especially with the historical way of thinking, which threatens acutely the basic notion that underlies this apologetic: the notion of miracle itself. The problem thus created cannot be solved by the deliberate paradox of a purely emotional affirmation of this apologetic, by the freethinking denial of all claims to religious truth, or by some kind of speculative middle course. A solution is to be found only by carrying to its conclusion—without any reservations—the historical way of thinking which gives evidence of this distinction between naïve and artificial absoluteness and which frees religious faith from inner adherence to the artificial kind by recognizing it as a relatively legitimate consequence of history.

This artificial apologetic is something intermediate between naïve, natural absoluteness and comparative or relational thinking that stops short after going a quarter or a half of the way. It does not matter whether such thinking is oriented to the popular religions of fantasy, imagery, and legend, or to thought conceived at a higher level that consciously strives for universality. It clings to an isolated point of departure understood only in its own light, a starting point in which the natural, naïve absoluteness of the objective reality is already entwined into the historical expression of the moment. Thinking of this kind does not even consider separating these two, for during the first flush of enthusiasm it is impossible to conceive of such a thing. Only subsequent, calmer reflection can give rise to the idea of separating naïve absoluteness from its historical expression. The result of thinking based on a mixture of the two is that the faithful find it impossible to experience the breadth, grandeur, and freedom that inspired the preaching of Jesus, for his message was conceived in the depths of his own soul, not fashioned out of the devotion or the experiences of believing disciples. The grandeur and power of the religious idea attach themselves to every word and image of the Master and endow them—and the thoughts that have directly or unconsciously become associated with them—with absolute authority. Ardor and love, with their natural desire for increase, do their best to remove everything ordinary and human from this authority. Then, even though the Christian position may be beset by attacks, doubts, hesitations, or alien and yet imposing ideas, it will not succumb to such threats but will stand even more firmly because of this authority that is understood with the full strength of inner compulsion and passionate devotion.

It becomes particularly important, therefore, for this authority to provide, in relation to such inner compulsion and devotion, a position free in principle from any possibility of attack or doubt, of supplementation or correction. Thus the first and most important formative idea takes shape: the idea of a revelation of the divine that is more than divine, being divine in such a way that absolutely no human attack or addition is conceivable. This is why, in the early church, there is no possibility of appraising alien or opposing positions as involving a relative legitimacy. They must all derive from the devil and the demons, or from human malice and folly. Only one's own position is regarded positively, all others being treated negatively, and this leads to a decisive and fundamental definition of relationship expressed in the controlling idea of *supernatural absoluteness*.

Given this idea, the Christian position may be confronted by philosophical speculations and systems of philosophy, by ethical forces and cultural developments to which it is in some degree inwardly related and in which it encounters truth that cannot be entirely denied; but even so, the relationship that ensues is not one of relative appreciation. Instead, whatever the Christian position can assimilate, or whatever it has an affinity for, is simply adopted as belonging to its own truth, as being its own offspring, or as directed to it by God. Conversely, everything that resists assimilation is disposed of as due to demonic or human duplicity.

Plato is turned into a plagiarist of Moses, while resemblances to Christianity in the religions and traditions of old are made out to be mockeries by which Satan seeks to lead Christians astray. Sin, the profound meaning of which Christianity had disclosed so forcefully, is made into a hereditary curse or fate of mankind that nullifies all goodness and knowledge of God outside Christianity. Idealistic movements of ethical and religious reform are explained as remnants of the primordial revelation that is first given rational articulation by the church.

Thus arises the second fundamental and decisive definition of relationship—*rational absoluteness.* From this vantage point it is declared that all truth prior to or outside Christianity is a remnant of the primordial revelation or a preparatory work of the Logos that became man in Christ. All such truth falls into an integrated and consistent, if limited, dimension of reality that is simply claimed by Christianity as flesh of its flesh, as identical with itself.

If the first idea takes shape in the pioneering labors and conflicts of the uncultured congregation, working, so to speak, in the shadows among the lower ranks of society, the second comes into being with Christianity's penetration into the strata of educated people and men of letters, with the emergence of an apologetic literature that lives in worldly forms and struggles with worldly questions. But the path to be followed in the subsequent theological development of these ideas is, in effect, already opened up.

There is a burgeoning of dogmatics and dogmatic thinking proper that takes a starting point removed from any control or analysis and combines it with every conceivable truth and idea. This process, however, is an unconscious one as far as the starting point itself is concerned. Intractable cases are sometimes denied outright, at other times simply absorbed. On this basis a general interpretation of reality is then projected, leading to the conclusion that this particular miracle-attested revelation must necessarily stand in antithesis to everything else human. A system of guarantees is developed that severs everything significant within the circle of revelation from everything profane. The entire history of ordinary occurrences is surrendered to weak and fallible human powers, but to this history is opposed a supernatural idea of history that reserves for itself the sacred sphere of miracle and revelation with its culmination in the codification of sacred truth and in the institution of a holy church. Ethical and religious forces outside this sphere are interpreted as nothing but natural achievements that stand under the ban of original sin; they are really only glittering vices. Absolute truth is surrounded with the institutions of the church and canon law, with the sacraments as the material and therefore unquestionably reliable bearers and guarantors of ecclesiastical grace and truth, and with a wall of sacred books, dogmas, creeds, rituals, and moral laws. Thus the whole, both theoretically and practically, is upheld on every side in its incomparable, exclusive truth.

In all this, the gulf between the absolute and the relative is thus made deeper and deeper, the relative becoming increasingly characterized as a morass of sin and error brightened by only a few sparks of truth. At the same time, however, the church carefully gathers all these tiny sparks together on her own sacred hearth, where they grow into a mighty flame. Everything true and noble that is conceived in metaphysics, cosmology, psychology, ethics, or statecraft, she draws to herself as a fragment and expression of her own truth and cultivates as an essential part of her own heritage. Thus all the great problems of mankind, and all skill in theoretical thinking, are claimed on behalf of the church, and it is by the church, and particularly because of her supernatural foundation, that they are rightly comprehended and brought to an authentic conclusion. Church philosophy constitutes the rational absoluteness of Christianity, just as the doctrines of the incarnation, revelation, and ecclesiology constitute the supernatural.

In this transformation of naïve absoluteness into one that is artificial, scholarly, and apologetic, Christianity does not stand alone—though in accordance with the unsurpassed religious energy at work in it, Christianity has perfected this absoluteness more than any other religion. Even the polytheistic ethnic religions, when their naïve absoluteness is assailed, construct general theories, learned explanations of their myths, and syncretistic equations of their gods with those of other peoples, thus buttressing their own faith amid the clash of ideas. It is the religions we refer to as world religions, however, which have produced apologetics that can be compared with one another and which have created organizations for their adherents that not only closely parallel the phenomenon of the Christian church but also depend on identical motives and processes.[4] On every hand natural absoluteness gradually grows beyond its naïve, self-contained outlook into a doctrine of unique and miraculous expressions of the divine. This doctrine is then opposed to other religions as the one and only truth, to individual deviations as orthodoxy, and to the questing intellectual life of reflection—whether exalted or profound—as the codification of divine wisdom. Sacred books, sacred dogmas, sacred laws, and materially demarcated and guaranteed means of grace everywhere circumscribe the heritage of the founding prophets. A developed theology—sometimes mythologizing, sometimes speculative—establishes a lasting relationship between this one and only truth and the manifestations of the religious life that encompass and adhere to it.

Indeed, the Christian apologetic is more than a mere parallel to these developments, for Christianity has to some extent adopted them from others and even elaborated them. It appropriated the Jewish theology of revelation and history as well as the Jewish doctrine of inspiration, using them to determine what value to assign to historical events and to key scriptures and laws. In particular, the Christian apologetic has received important influences from the incarnation theories with which the syncretistic mysteries and speculations gave apologetic support to their esoteric doctrines. The high point of this kind of borrowing was reached in the Middle Ages when the Christian apologetic took over from Jewish and Islamic theology the idea of interpreting Aristotle as a complement of natural reason to the supernatural authority of dogma.

As a matter of fact, the parallel between Christianity and other world religions extends well into the sphere of cognate theories of religious absoluteness. All the ideal elements of life, though rightly felt to be expressions of the necessary when first manifested, are later consolidated into theories that make what was perceived as necessary in experience into something theoretically necessary, immutable, and fixed. Furthermore, such theories provide support for dogmatic thought (in the philosophical sense of the term) by working out a doctrine of society, aesthetics, logic, metaphysics, and particularly ethics. The theological and the philosophical temper are closely related. They spring from the same psychological soil. The theory of absoluteness took shape in an intellectual atmosphere in which a dogmatic way of thinking dominated other disciplines as well, and that is why it could acquire the firm relationship with them that has in fact endured.

Artificial absoluteness is, in short, a theoretical determination of relationship in which the only fixed point is its starting point in personal or inherited faith. All else is regarded strictly in terms of that one point, being brought into definite relation with it either by absorption or by rejection. Artificial absoluteness results from a process of comparison and contrast which, due to the determinative influence of naïve absoluteness, is itself relatively naïve at first. That is to say, at the beginning of this process great care is exercised as to the factors admitted into relationship. Men content themselves with simple, vivid representations as produced by reflection and imagination. In time this absoluteness grows and evolves into an all-inclusive theory. Thus artificial absoluteness results from contrast, comparison, and reflection— and ultimately from formal scholarship. It leads, in Catholicism, to the Thomistic system with its practical complement in the infallibility of the Pope, and in Protestantism to a dogmatics which combines natural and supernatural illumination and finds its practical support in the inspiration of the Bible.

However, the ideas of comparison, combination, contrast, and fusion that were thus adopted and developed in the discipline of dogmatic theology cannot be arrested at this stage. They press beyond previously maintained dogmatic presuppositions to comparisons and interconnections that are constantly being renewed, expanded, and reconceived with regard to the basic principles on which they depend. The components to be compared and related become increasingly numerous and more radical, while their common point of reference gradually frees itself from what is dogmatically guaranteed as objective and presses upward toward the center of the whole. Sometimes this leads to providing supernatural theories with even stronger supports, rational grounds being given for what is in principle an anti-rational position. At other times the dogmatic *ratio* permeates every corner of theology and rationalizes it so thoroughly that it contradicts its original meaning. Fundamentally new metaphysical, cosmological, and psychological theories arise, and the outer ramparts are assigned to these in order that the main fortress may be better protected. Again, epistemological inquiries are undertaken that call into question the whole basis upon which thinking has previously taken place, and such inquiries pose a threat to our fundamental concepts as to the object of theological reflection.

Eventually, the new understanding of the world developed on the basis of science collides with the old one of the Bible and church philosophy. One effect of this collision is that the apologetic, supernatural idea of history can no longer prevent the secular idea of history from trespassing on its territory.

This last development is attended by the most momentous consequences, for it threatens not only the substance of theological doctrines but the very foundations upon which the venture of dogmatic theology, even in its rationalized forms, ordinarily depends. This is where the hottest battle ensues and where the most astounding concessions take place. Theology makes its investigation of sacred events conform, point for point, to the methods by which secular events are investigated. This leads, first, to the acknowledgment of a resemblance between the religions of past and present, between the rise of religious literature and that of secular writings, and between Christian and non-Christian religions. This requires in turn a completely new understanding of the religious developments which entered into the historical situation that Christianity belonged to at the time of its origin and which have influenced it, directly and indirectly, in many ways. And this calls for a universal history of religion with its various types of absoluteness and its different churches, dogmas, sacred writings, revelations, and theologies.

Confronted by this state of affairs, Christian thinkers of the modern era have discarded the old methods by which the artificial absoluteness of the ecclesiastical apologetic had been maintained, methods that combined the doctrine of miracle with the doctrine of revelation and the theory of a natural knowledge of God with the doctrine of original sin. They acknowledged history in all its length and breadth, both in its common features and in the forward strides for which there is no precedent or parallel, as the basis of theological thinking. Men now sought to work out speculative interpretations of history, at first timorously and in accordance with the ideas of the early church—as in Deism—but then boldly and with originality, as in the philosophy of history of German idealism since Lessing and Herder.

Thus supernatural and rational absoluteness gave rise to *evolutionary absoluteness*. Its expounders, having a heightened understanding of the antitheses to be overcome, formulated the problem more sharply than before and coined the term "absoluteness" to express it. It was in this context that Christianity, previously interpreted as unique and supernaturally revealed truth, became in the true sense of the term the absolute religion: the religion which exhausts the essence of its creative principle, the realization of the idea of religion. What was sacrificed on the one hand to the position of formal uniqueness asserted by orthodox dogmatics was, on the other hand, substantially enriched in the working out of this concept. The truth spoken of in these terms is no longer merely a truth which, being knowable in incarnation, miracle, and prophecy, is absolutely certain but not yet exhaustive. Now it is the perfect truth that exhausts its principle, the truth that merely needs to purify its eternal principle from the forms by which it is historically actualized and mediated.

This excessive emphasis on perfection and its fundamental divergence from the preaching of Jesus—for whom all ultimate salvation and all ultimate truth were primarily something to be awaited—show, however, that what we are dealing with here is actually an artificial absoluteness. The artificial character of this absoluteness becomes most evident when this concept is applied to actual history. Real history recognizes only individual and temporary structures that are related to their goal strictly in terms of a tendency toward the absolute. This puts an end to all the reservations, provisos, and limitations presupposed in a Christian supernaturalism which was expendable from the outset and which had the effect of fettering theologically oriented historical research while at the same time lightening its task. Even this last form of artificial absoluteness shatters under the impact of real history.

This brings us back to our starting point. The theme central to this concluding section of our inquiry has now been examined from every relevant angle, and it should now be possible to suggest an answer to the question with which we began and in doing so to resolve the misgivings formulated above as well.

Only superficial acquaintance with science can estrange men from God, and only a superficial understanding of history can lead men to believe that religion must fade away because of the apparent contradictoriness of its different kinds of absoluteness. Study of history that does not stop short with mere facts but seeks out their interconnections will discern in these various claims to absoluteness the contextually appropriate expression of the absoluteness of the goal toward which they are oriented. Within each religion this goal is naïvely perceived in terms of its substantive, inner imperative, and it remains confined within the perspectives of naïve understanding as long as it is not compared with other religions. Till such comparison takes place, the temporary position that any given religion maintains with regard to its knowledge of the higher life seems ultimate and unique. Thus these naïve claims to absoluteness present themselves to us as interrelated but meaningfully different facets of the religious phenomenon, their differences corresponding to the degree of strength and clarity with which the religious goal stands over against the world with positively liberating and redeeming power.

Just as Christianity is the only religion that fully perfects this contrast in principle, so too its claim to absoluteness is inwardly the freest and most universal. Its claim binds the inmost self to the spirit of its founder and not to a written code. The limitations associated with the naïve outlook cling to the Christian claim to absoluteness in two ways: first, in the identification of the Christian claim with the original, individual, historical figure who is the source of its religious orientation (especially evident in the expectation of the last judgment); and second, in the notion that the validity of Christianity is wholly self-derived, other truths being totally disregarded. It is important, to be sure, to do away with these limitations, for history itself has already annihilated them in principle. It is necessary to do away with fixation on a single point, not only because the movement of history has carried us beyond that point but also because historical knowledge has taught us to see it in terms of its position within a system of development. What is decisive, therefore, is no longer the claim to absoluteness but the reality reflected in the nature and strength of the claim—the religious and ethical world of thought and life itself. The validity of Christianity is verified not by arguing the nature and strength of claims to revelation, redemption, and truth but by judging what lies behind the claim. But if what is substantive takes the place of the claim, it likewise follows that the relativity and similarity found in the claims of the various religions cannot threaten Christianity. Indeed, one may even venture to suggest that there is a correspondence between the uniqueness of what lies behind a claim and a unique form of the claim to absoluteness. What is essential, however, is the former, not the latter.[5]

This conclusion should satisfy the Christian sense of what it means to lead a religiously and ethically involved life, not merely as an inevitable concession to science but as its own inner demand. What is substantive can be disengaged from its form as a claim to absoluteness, the form in which it made its first naïve appearance and which was then artificially theorized. If prophetic and Christian personalism is valid, then the course it follows toward the absolute is certain and its superiority over other paths is sure. Its essentially Christian character is assured, even though it is detached from older theories of revelation and redemption, of original sin and exclusive truth. By virtue of this disengage-ment, Christian personalism enters freely and vigorously into the perspectives of the modern understanding of the world.[6]

The artificial absoluteness of the older apologetic possessed great comforting and elevating power when it existed within a dogmatic intellectual atmosphere as a simple extension and elab-oration of natural absoluteness. Even in that context, however, the all-too-human frailties that clung to it—contention and rancor, arrogance and spiritual oppression—were often appalling. In an atmosphere of critical and historical thought like that of today, this artificial absoluteness has become even more of a burden to Christian self-understanding. Clerical ferocity and theological subtlety make artificial absoluteness increasingly op-pressive. The dedicated efforts of devout and profound teachers only make it more venerable, not more bearable.

But if it is scientific study of history that has made this burden so onerous, it is also scientific study of history that frees men from this burden when it is thought through to the end. Then we discover the distinction between naïve absoluteness and artificial, apologetic absoluteness, a distinction rooted in the very nature of the matter and actually a phenomenon common to all the higher religions. Apologetic absoluteness becomes plainly recognizable for what it is because of its natural divergence from naïve absoluteness and because of the gradual disintegration that results when it embraces elements for which it has an affinity and then tries to buttress its position in those terms. On the other hand, it is because of this self-induced disintegration that artificial absoluteness leads us deeper and deeper into history and enables us to perceive the sources of artificial absoluteness in their origi-nal, naïve forms. We are also led to see the disparity between the naïve absoluteness of Christianity and the claims in which the truth of the lower-ranking religions is disclosed. Thus artificial absoluteness leads us to distinguish Jesus' message from every early Christian or ecclesiastical apologetic. It leads us back to the grandeur, breadth, and freedom of Jesus, whose message remains the highest and greatest we know.

At this juncture, however, we are grasped by the authority of

Jesus himself, to whom, as the highest religious power, we may in good conscience devote ourselves with such reverence and commitment that we forget about all the wearisome roads and detours apart from which a people enmeshed in the diversity of history cannot come to him. The religious man can and may forget the study of history at this point and live with naïve absoluteness in the presence of God, all time being consumed in the vision of the One disclosed to us as the divine goal. Insofar as reinforcement from history and from the great religious personalities is needed, and especially insofar as a visualization of its foundations is indispensable to the cohesiveness and propagation of a religious community as well as to the very possibility of organized worship, the religious man will turn back to history and to these personalities; but he will not let critical historical scholarship interfere with that visualizing of history whose sole intention is to serve the edification and deepening of the spiritual life. The more thoroughly it does justice to history scientifically, the more unrestrainedly will naïve absoluteness make use of historical traditions that are intrinsically significant to it.[7]

However much the figure of Jesus may be concealed under early Christian apologetics or dogmatic systems based on naïve traditions, it is plainly evident that what constantly radiates from him is the marvelous spontaneity with which he expressed so simply what is highest and most profound, connecting this in the most natural way with the belief that he had been sent by the Father. When the clouds of research have lifted, this final result will remain forever, and he who sympathetically involves himself with the diverse truths and values of mankind and seeks his way accordingly will discover in this completely free spontaneity, which is at the same time the expression of the purest and most concentrated religious power, an indication of the highest revelation of the divine life that holds sway over us. He will not deny the naïve limitations of even this claim to absoluteness, and he will not recoil when this religious orientation, developing close connections with new ideas, enters into new forms of existence. The fragmentariness and incompleteness of our knowledge, even today, make it plain that these new relationships too will have to be understood in terms of their historical limitations. In all this, he will simply live out of God's resources and in the presence of God, leading in his own way the life bestowed on us by Jesus and for which Jesus' struggle and victory constantly give us new strength and courage.

On the other hand, such a man will not seek to buttress this faith in such a way as to establish an impassable gulf between it and all other faiths or to deny the salvation that others have received. He will, however, feel constrained to lead others to the higher clarity of the salvation he knows. Again, he will not seek to filter out of the history of Christianity a finished and permanent principle of religion. Instead, he will rely upon the guiding hand of God, who leads us historically within history, and will leave to Jesus the disclosure and consummation of the salvation of the future.

We need not fret over unknown thousands of centuries of human history. It is enough if we can throw light on the next stretch of the path and if we know now what we want to be and should be. What is called for at this moment of history is to resist the religious chaos and religious devastation that threaten us from every side.

In conclusion it may now be said without fear of contradiction that the standpoint represented here need not fall back on abandoned theories in order to affirm its Christian character or sacrifice its Christian character in order to draw out correctly the consequences of its historical perspective. It differentiates itself in many ways from the theology that preceded it, but it also presupposes a radical change in our situation as a whole, including the modern historical horizon and modern genetic thought. This is not a matter of making adjustments at a few isolated points. Our entire outlook must be directed to new questions. These are not, of course, the only questions that should be solved today by those who perceive in Christian personalism the inalienable heritage of our religious and intellectual existence as over against all the pantheistic and relativistic tendencies of the modern spirit. The natural sciences of the modern era require an equally comprehensive recasting of their world view, which is still to some extent influenced by the early Christian and medieval world view. Here too the theologians, if they take the problem seriously at all, think that they may be able to help in a small way. But that is not the point to be stressed here. Our concern is with the effects of modern historical thinking. These effects are far-reaching and call for a rethinking of every aspect of the religious phenomenon, but they do not destroy Christian personalism or the confidence men have in the unique and sublime path by which it leads them to the absolute.

One must embrace the whole in order to win the whole. What will become of our ecclesiastical, more or less liberalized systems of dogmatics, and of the actual church situations most immediately related to them, is a problem in its own right. At this point the most difficult developments of the future lie before us, and they cannot be regulated with understanding or certainty unless we desire and attain full theoretical clarity as to the situation in the Christian world of thought. The inevitable concessions and compromises will follow of themselves, but they ought not to be the primary goal of theology.

NOTES

Foreword to the First Edition

1. Adolf von Harnack, *Die Aufgabe der theologischen Fakultäten und die allgemeine Religionsgeschichte* (Giessen, 1901). [Later reprinted in Harnack's *Reden und Aufsätze*, 2. Aufl., Band 2 (Giessen, 1906), 159–187.]

2. Adolf Jülicher, *Moderne Meinungsverschiedenheiten über Methoden, Aufgaben und Ziele der Kirchengeschichte* (Marburg, 1901).

3. Carl Albrecht Bernoulli, *Die wissenschaftliche und die kirchliche Methode in der Theologie* (Freiburg, 1897).

4. Georg Wobbermin, "Das Verhältnis der Theologie zur modernen Wissenschaft und ihre Stellung im Gesamtrahmen der Wissenschaften," *Zeitschrift für Theologie und Kirche*, 10. Jahrgang (1900), 375–438.

5. Friedrich Traub, "Die religionsgeschichtliche Methode und die systematische Theologie," *Zeitschrift für Theologie und Kirche*, 11. Jahrgang (1901), 301–340.

6. Max Reischle, "Historische und dogmatische Methode der Theologie," *Theologische Rundschau*, 4. Jahrgang (1901), 261–275, 305–324.

7. Richard Adelbert Lipsius, *Lehrbuch der evangelisch-protestantischen Dogmatik*, 3. Aufl. (Braunschweig, 1893).

8. Ludwig Ihmels, *Die Selbständigkeit der Dogmatik gegenüber der Religionsphilosophie* (Leipzig, 1901).

9. Carl Friedrich Georg Heinrici, *Dürfen wir noch Christen bleiben?* (Leipzig, 1901).

10. Ernst Troeltsch, "Die Selbständigkeit der Religion," *Zeitschrift für Theologie und Kirche*, 5. Jahrgang (1895), 361–436; 6. Jahrgang (1896), 71–110 and 167–218. See especially 5. Jahrgang (1895), pp. 400, 402, 434, 436.

11. Gustav Theodor Fechner, *Die drei Motive und Gründe des Glaubens* (Leipzig, 1863).

12. Troeltsch, *op. cit.*, 6. Jahrgang (1896), 102.

13. Rudolf Eucken, *Der Wahrheitsgehalt der Religion* (Leipzig, 1901). (Eng. trans. by W. Tudor Jones entitled *The Truth of Religion*, from the third German edition of 1912 [London and New York, 1913].)

14. *Kant's Gesammelte Schriften*, herausgegeben von der königlich preussischen Akademie der Wissenschaften. Band 10: *Briefwechsel* (Berlin, 1900), 152–153. (The parenthesized word is an addition by Troeltsch, and the italics are his also.)

15. *Friedrich Schleiermacher's Sämmtliche Werke*, Band 12: *Die christliche Sitte . . .*, herausgegeben von L. Jonas (Berlin, 1843), 302–303. (Schleiermacher italicized all of what Troeltsch cites here.)

16. Ihmels, *op. cit.*, 7.

Foreword to the Second Edition

1. Wilhelm Herrmann, review in the *Theologische Literaturzeitung*, 27. Jahrgang (1902), 330–334.

2. Paul Jäger, review in *Die Christliche Welt* (1902), 914–921, 930–942.

3. Rudolf Eucken, review in the *Göttingische gelehrte Anzeigen*, 165. Jahrgang (1903), 177–186.

4. Johannes Thomä, *Die Absolutheit des Christentums* (Leipzig, 1907).

5. Friedrich Brunstäd, *Ueber die Absolutheit des Christentums* (1905).

6. Karl Beth, "Das Wesen des Christentums und die historische Forschung," *Neue kirchliche Zeitschrift*, 15. Jahrgang (1904).

7. Carl Friedrich Georg Heinrici, *Theologie und Religionswissenschaft* (Leipzig, 1902).

8. August Wilhelm Hunzinger, "Die religionsphilosophische Aufgabe der kirchlichen Theologie," *Neue kirchliche Zeitschrift*, 18. Jahrgang (1907).

9. A. W. Hunzinger, *Probleme und Aufgaben der gegenwärtigen systematischen Theologie* (Leipzig, 1909).

10. Ludwig Ihmels, "Blicke in die neuere dogmatische Arbeit," *Neue kirchliche Zeitschrift*, 16. Jahrgang (1905), 505–522.

11. Wilhelm Bousset, "Kantisch-Friessche Religionsphilosophie und ihre Anwendung auf die Theologie," *Theologische Rundschau*, 12. Jahrgang (1909), 419–436, 471–488.

12. Eduard Spranger, *Die Grundlagen der Geschichtswissenschaft* (Berlin, 1905).

13. Theodor Kaftan, *Ernst Troeltsch, eine kritische Zeitstudie* (Schleswig, 1912).

14. Rudolf Eucken, *Hauptprobleme der Religionsphilosophie der Gegenwart* (Berlin, 1909).

15. Paul Wernle, *Einführung in das theologische Studium* (Tübingen, 1908).

16. Ernst Troeltsch, "Die Bedeutung des Begriffes der Kontingenz," *Zeitschrift für Theologie und Kirche*, 20. Jahrgang (1910), 421–430. (Later reprinted in Troeltsch's *Gesammelte Schriften*, Band 2 [Tübingen, 1913], 769–778; Eng. trans. under the title "Contingency" in James Hastings, ed., *Encyclopaedia of Religion and Ethics*, Vol. 4 [Edinburgh and New York, 1911], 87–89.)

17. Troeltsch, "Die Mission in der modernen Welt," *Die Christliche Welt*, 20. Jahrgang (1906). (Reprinted in Ernst Troeltsch, *Gesammelte Schriften*, Band 2 [Tübingen, 1913], 779–804.)

18. Troeltsch, "Missionsmotiv, Missionsaufgabe und neuzeitliches Humanitätschristentum," *Zeitschrift für Missionskunde und Religionswissenschaft*, 22. Jahrgang (1907), 129–139, 161–166.

19. Troeltsch, *Die Bedeutung der Geschichtlichkeit Jesu für den Glauben* (Tübingen, 1911).

20. Troeltsch, *Soziallehren der christlichen Kirchen und Gruppen* (Tübingen, 1912). (Eng. trans. by Olive Wyon entitled *The Social Teaching of the Christian Churches* [London and New York, 1931], currently available as a paperback from Harper and Row, New York.)

CHAPTER 1

1. Cf. Wilhelm Windelband, *Geschichte und Naturwissenschaft* [History and Natural Science] (Strassburg, 1894); Heinrich Rickert, *Die Grenzen der naturwissenschaftlichen Begriffsbildung* [The Limitations of Forming Concepts according to the Model of the Natural Sciences], 1. Hälfte (Freiburg, 1896); *Idem.*, *Kulturwissenschaft und Naturwissenschaft* [The Study of Human Culture and the Study of Nature] (Freiburg, 1899); *Idem.*, "Les quatre modes de l' «Universel» en histoire" [The Four Modes of Universality in History], *Revue de synthèse historique*, Tome 2 (1901), 121–140; Georg Simmel, *Probleme der Geschichtsphilosophie* [Problems in the Philosophy of History] (Leipzig, 1892); Wilhelm Dilthey, *Ideen über eine beschreibende und zergliedernde Psychologie* [Ideas concerning a Descriptive and Analytical Psychology] (Berlin, 1894);

Hugo Münsterberg, *Grundzüge der Psychologie* [Basic Elements of Psychology],
Band 1 (Leipzig, 1900). The criticism of the last book in this list expressed by
Otto Ritschl in his *Die Causalbetrachtung in den Geisteswissenschaften* [The
View of Causality in the Human Sciences] (Bonn, 1901) I can apply to myself
only as regards my adherence to the concept of types. Cf. also Rudolf Eucken,
Die Einheit des Geisteslebens in Bewusstsein und Tat der Menschheit [The
Unity of Human Life in the Consciousness and Behavior of Mankind] (Leipzig,
1888). Finally, cf. my works *Ueber historische und dogmatische Methode in der
Theologie* [The Historical vs. the Dogmatic Method in Theology] (Tübingen,
1900) [later reprinted in Ernst Troeltsch, *Gesammelte Schriften*, Band 2
(Tübingen, 1913), 729–753] and the articles in J. J. Herzog's *Realencyklopädie*,
3. Aufl. (24 vols., Leipzig, 1896–1913) entitled "Aufklärung" [The Enlighten-
ment], Band 2 (1897), 225–241, "Deutscher Idealismus" [German Idealism],
Band 8 (1900), 612–637, and "Deismus" [Deism], Band 4 (1898), 532–559, in
which I have thrown some light on the historical development of the modern
approach to history. Subsequently I have continued these inquiries in my
book *Das Historische in Kants Religionsphilosophie* [The Historical in Kant's
Philosophy of Religion] (Berlin, 1904). An important aspect of the problem
has been clarified by Arvid Grotenfelt, *Die Wertschätzung in der Geschichte*
[Value Assessment in History] (Leipzig, 1903) and by Julius Goldstein, *Die
empiristische Geschichtsauffassung David Humes* . . . [David Hume's Empirical
Conception of History] (Leipzig, 1902). Lastly, see also Walther Köhler, *Idee
und Persönlichkeit in der Kirchengeschichte* [Idea and Personality in Church
History] (Heft 61 in the *Sammlung ausserdeutscher Strafgesetzbücher*, Berlin,
1910).

2. Apart from Ferdinand Christian Baur's splendid work, the principles
of which were developed in the introduction to his *Das Christentum und die
christliche Kirche der drei ersten Jahrhunderte* [Christianity and the Christian
Church of the First Three Centuries], 2. Aufl. (Tübingen, 1860), one recalls
first of all Edward Caird's *The Evolution of Religion*, 2nd ed. (Glasgow, 1894)
and Otto Pfleiderer's *Religionsphilosophie auf geschichtlicher Grundlage*
[Philosophy of Religion on a Historical Basis], 3. Aufl. (Berlin, 1896). Both of
these books are excellent in their own way. For special application to Christianity and the person of Jesus, the works of Karl Theodor Keim, which are
always worthy of attention, are significant—especially the dogmatic and philosophical use he makes of these works in his *Der geschichtliche Christus* [The
Historical Christ], 2. Aufl. (Zürich, 1865). Schleiermacher's and Hegel's theories
on the philosophy of history and the study of religion, despite the abundance
of writings about them, have not yet, to my knowledge, found expression or
application proceeding from more comprehensive points of view. For the most
part the state of knowledge of the extremely important teachings of German
idealism, particularly those relating to the understanding of history and the
philosophy of development, is still very poor, even though it is precisely the
theologians who have the greatest need of understanding the principles operative in their work. Meanwhile we have such works as: Georg Wehrung, *Der
geschichtsphilosophische Standpunkt Schleiermachers zur Zeit seiner Freund-
schaft mit den Romantikern* [Schleiermacher's Point of View regarding the
Philosophy of History up to the Time of His Friendship with the Romantics]
(Strassburg, 1907); Idem., *Die philosophisch-theologische Methode Schleiermachers* [Schleiermacher's Philosophical and Theological Method] (Göttingen,
1911); and Hermann Süskind, *Christentum und Geschichte bei Schleiermacher*
[Christianity and History according to Schleiermacher] (Tübingen, 1911).
Schleiermacher's way of thinking, in the *Glaubenslehre* [The Christian Faith]
of his churchly period, is ultimately a very refracted one. The greater consistency
on Hegel's part is unmistakable. Significant works have now appeared on

Hegel's philosophy of history. The problems are outlined by Emil Lask, *Fichtes Idealismus und die Geschichte* [Fichte's Idealism and History] (Tübingen, 1902), and are admirably developed by Wilhelm Dilthey, *Die Jugendgeschichte Hegels* [Hegel as a Young Man] (Berlin, 1905). (Later reprinted in *Wilhelm Diltheys Gesammelte Schriften* [Leipzig, 1921–1924], Band 4.)

3. In the last analysis this is the tendency and achievement of the theology of Frank, who represents in my opinion the most brilliant, profound, and lucid development of modern orthodoxy. Cf. the above-mentioned essay by Ludwig Ihmels and his larger book *Die christliche Wahrheitsgewissheit, ihr letzter Grund und ihre Entstehung* [The Christian Certainty of Truth: Its Ultimate Foundation and Its Development] (Leipzig, 1901). At bottom his work signifies the reduction of supernatural assurance to immanent, psychological factors. On this basis one is expected to arrive at transeunt factors of a metaphysical or historical kind, the miraculous works of God in innately sinful man, and the miraculous revelation of the salvific acts attested in the Bible. But it is precisely this last, decisive application which is the most difficult. Ihmels holds that Frank leaves the problem hanging in midair and attempts to work out a more satisfactory solution. That he has any possibility of succeeding is a point I am not prepared to concede. It is significant that similar attempts are emerging in Catholic theology as well, including arguments based on the impossibility of employing external, historical proofs of authority. Cf. Lucien Laberthonnière, "L'Apologétique et la méthode de Pascal" [Pascal's Apologetic and Method] in the *Revue du clergé français*, Tome 25 (Déc. 1900–Fév. 1901), 472–498. At this point such thinkers associate themselves with Pascal, and in instructive agreement with the terminology of Frank, the author designates his method as *la méthode de l'immanence*. Even such admirable systematic theologies as those of Beck and Kähler depend, ultimately, on the same basic ideas. Cf. my review of Martin Kähler, *Dogmatischen Zeitfragen* [Theological Questions of Contemporary Relevance] (Leipzig, 1898) in the *Göttingische gelehrte Anzeigen*, 161. Jahrgang (1899), 942–952. Kähler's paradoxical position with regard to research into the message of Jesus illuminates the difficulties this approach has with history, difficulties which in his case merely make their appearance at different points than in the case of Frank.

4. Cf., in this connection, my debate with Julius Kaftan entitled "Geschichte und Metaphysik" [History and Metaphysics], *Zeitschrift für Theologie und Kirche*, 8. Jahrgang (1898), 1–69. The strongly Hegelian standpoint that appeared in that article has here been transformed into a critical one, due to the influence of Rickert. See also my discussion with Rickert entitled "Moderne Geschichtsphilosophie" [Modern Philosophy of History], *Theologische Rundschau*, 6. Jahrgang (1903), 3–28, 57–72, 103–117. (Later reprinted in Troeltsch, *Gesammelte Schriften*, Band 2 [Tübingen, 1913], 673–728.)

5. Cf. my *Die wissenschaftliche Lage und ihre Anforderungen an die Theologie* [The Intellectual Situation and What It Requires of Theology] (Freiburg, 1900), 13–27. It would be a profitable task to describe the encounter between early Christian theology and the non-Christian religions and to indicate what utilization of the early intellectual interpretations of myth followed from this encounter. With reference to the philosophy of history held by the early Christians, see Adolf von Harnack, *Die Mission und Ausbreitung des Christentums in den ersten drei Jahrhunderten* [The Mission and Expansion of Christianity in the First Three Centuries] (Leipzig, 1902), 177–179.

6. For the first theory, cf. the instructive book by Johannes Steinbeck, *Verhältnis von Theologie und Erkenntnistheorie* [The Relationship between Theology and Epistemology] (Leipzig, 1899), which is important for understanding this position as a whole. The impossibility of proving inner miracle to be truly miraculous was shown as long ago as Duns Scotus, in his critique

of the *habitus supernaturalis*, which he opposed to the external miracle of the Church and her authority. (See Reinhold Seeberg, *Die Theologie des Duns Scotus* [The Theology of Duns Scotus] [Band 5 of *Studien zur Geschichte der Theologie und der Kirche*, edited by N. Bonwetsch and R. Seeberg (Leipzig, 1900)], 130, 310.) Also, the encyclical *Pascendi* opposes above all else basing religious knowledge on the *immanentia vitalis* or *immanentia religiosa* because they imperil miracle and therewith the basis of absoluteness generally. (See Alfred Loisy, *Simples réflexions* [Paris, 1908], 16 f.) For the second theory, cf. Harnack, *Das Wesen des Christentums* [The Essence of Christianity], 4. Aufl. (Leipzig, 1901), 41: "It is evident, then, that the Gospel is not a positive religion like the others, that it has nothing legalistic or particularistic about it, that *it is therefore religion itself*" [Harnack's italics]. Likewise page 44, and especially in the address entitled *Die Aufgabe der theologischen Fakultäten und die allgemeine Religionsgeschichte* [The Task of Theological Faculties and the General History of Religion] (Giessen, 1901), 15–16: "One concerns himself with religion universally if he concerns himself with Christianity." [Cf. Harnack, *Reden und Aufsätze*, 2. Aufl., Band 2 (Giessen, 1906), 174.] It is because of statements such as these that heresy-hunting ignorance has spoken of Harnack's "deism."

CHAPTER 2

1. Cf. my criticism of the concept of evolution in "Die Selbständigkeit der Religion" [The Independence of Religion], *Zeitschrift für Theologie und Kirche*, 6. Jahrgang (1896), 178–183, and in my review of August Johannes Dorner, *Grundriss der Dogmengeschichte* [Outline of the History of Christian Teaching] (Berlin, 1899) in the *Göttingische gelehrte Anzeigen*, 163. Jahrgang (1901), 265–275; see also Emil Lask, *Fichtes Idealismus und die Geschichte* [Fichte's Idealism and History] (Tübingen, 1902), 56–68.

2. In support of this account I simply refer to the above-mentioned articles by my critics. The first is Wobbermin's interpretation (cf. *Zeitschrift für Theologie und Kirche*, 10. Jahrgang, 1900, 417, 421, 423), the second, Traub's (cf. especially *Zeitschrift für Theologie und Kirche*, 11. Jahrgang, 1901, 314–317), which is quite similar to Reischle's. It frequently happens in these theories that an approach to Christianity like the one developed in the present book is interpreted as obstinate with regard to its motives and blind as to its possibilities of self-deception. Moreover, to this approach is attributed, as its real motive, a certain *sense of assurance* which, though acknowledged as logically coherent, is characterized as something that is in the last analysis chronologically prior (Traub, 317; Reischle, 321) and discrete, an assurance based on a "specifically Christian certainty" in the sense described above. Against this intepretation I can only reply with equal obstinacy that such a "Christian epistemology" without the "Christian causality" that belongs to it strikes me as an artificial, incomplete sort of thing. If abandoned, it permits the development of a plain and natural view of the great rival types of religion, a balanced attitude toward them, and the establishment of this attitude on the theory of a common if differently realized goal. In a time of religious crisis like our own, pursuit of other types of religion is not merely a game that scholars play but is often a matter of serious, inner concern, and deciding between religions often involves real inner upheavals. The decision itself finally depends, of course, on an axiomatic attitude, but this attitude is nonetheless a result of extensive examination of the religions. Those involved seek a broad foundation in a concept of universality on the basis of which men who have some feeling for and understanding of the religious life can communicate with one another. It is in this way that an attitude toward differing spiritual values takes shape, and here nobody constructs exact theories of certainty which will

guarantee in advance that one particular type of spiritual life will emerge as supreme. Indeed, an outlook of the kind proposed here should be especially compatible with a theology that has accustomed us to understanding religion in its practical features and in its antithesis to philosophical theorems, thereby making necessary for us, as reference points for considering religion scientifically, not such philosophical principles as allegedly reside in the natural reason but rather the phenomena that are actually most closely related to it, namely, the other religions. In this connection one of the unintended consequences of this claim-theology (*Anspruchstheologie*) is that comparisons between Jesus and other founders of religion and their claims excite great interest for the reason that such comparisons are based on a real relationship. If, in Jesus' case, it is less the claim than its substance that calls for consideration, it follows that one will not "seek to understand Jesus by way of a detour around Zoroaster," a procedure which Jülicher ridiculed in his *Moderne Meinungsverschiedenheiten über Methoden, Aufgaben und Ziele der Kirchengeschichte* [Contemporary Differences of Opinion as to the Methods, Tasks, and Goals of Church History] (Marburg, 1901), p. 16.

CHAPTER 3

1. The exposition which follows on pages 86–102 has been reprinted in the reader *Moderne Philosophie*, ed. by Max Frischeisen-Köhler (Stuttgart, 1907), together with portions of Nietzsche's essay "Vom Nachteil der Historie für das Leben" [On the Disadvantage of History for Life]. Both pieces are intended to illustrate the problems of historicism.

2. Cf., on this point, the doctrine of "creative synthesis" proposed by Wilhelm Wundt (who in my opinion is still closely associated with naturalism), *System der Philosophie* [A System of Philosophy], 2. Aufl. (Leipzig, 1897), 596; moreover, in addition to the already cited works by Rickert, the second edition of his *Der Gegenstand der Erkenntnis* [The Object of Knowledge], 2. Aufl. (Tübingen, 1904), with his distinction between the causality that is subject to universal laws and individual causality (pp. 212–216); also his essay on "Psychophysische Causalität und psychophysischen Parallelismus" [Psycho-Physical Causality and Psycho-Physical Parallelism] in the *Philosophische Abhandlungen* [Philosophical Essays] (Tübingen, 1900) dedicated to Christoph Sigwart. Most important, however, see the extremely interesting works by Henri Bergson, *Essai sur les données immédiates de la conscience* (Paris, 1901) (Eng. trans. by F. L. Pogson entitled *Time and Free Will: An Essay on the Immediate Data of Consciousness* [New York, 1910]); *Materie und Gedächtnis* (Jena, 1908) (a German translation of *Matière et Mémoire* [Paris, 1896]; also translated into English by Nancy Margaret Paul and W. Scott Palmer as *Matter and Memory* [New York, 1911]); and *Évolution créatrice* (Paris, 1907) (Eng. trans. by Arthur Mitchell entitled *Creative Evolution* [New York, 1911]).

3. Cf. my article "Christentum und Geschichte" [Christianity and History], *Preussische Jahrbücher*, Band 87 (1897), 415–447. (Reprinted in Troeltsch, *Gesammelte Schriften*, Band 2 [Tübingen, 1913], 328–363.)

4. Cf. my "Selbständigkeit der Religion" [Independence of Religion], *Zeitschrift für Theologie und Kirche*, 5. Jahrgang (1895), 420–422.

5. With this conclusion my earlier comments on "Die Selbständigkeit der Religion" [The Independence of Religion] and "Geschichte und Metaphysik" [History and Metaphysics] (*Zeitschrift für Theologie und Kirche*, 8. Jahrgang, 1898, 1–69) are simply extended and in part more precisely defined in that a clearer break is made with the ideal of a religious principle than was the case even in the articles mentioned above. For the rest I refer readers to Rudolf Eucken's book *Der Wahrheitsgehalt der Religion* (Leipzig, 1901) [*The Truth of Religion*, translated by W. Tudor Jones, London and New York, 1913],

which comes quite close to my views. In my opinion, however, even Eucken disposes of the problem of absoluteness too abruptly. Yet his own exposition undermines the presuppositions of any such construction since it is dominated by the idea of a goal which comes into view in encounter with what is actually given in nature and provides an orienting beacon for future developments. In such encounters, however, this goal finds that its way is prepared and assured in principle only, but it never arrives at complete realization. Cf. further Eucken's *Können wir noch Christen sein?* [Can We Still Be Christians?] (Leipzig, 1911).

CHAPTER 4

1. Cf. my essay "Was heisst 'Wesen des Christentums'?" [What Is the Meaning of "The Essence of Christianity"?], *Die Christliche Welt*, 17. Jahrgang (1903) [later in Troeltsch, *Gesammelte Schriften*, Band 2 (Tübingen, 1913), 386–451].

2. Cf. "Die Selbständigkeit der Religion" [The Independence of Religion], *Zeitschrift für Theologie und Kirche*, 6. Jahrgang (1896), 186–205.

CHAPTER 5

1. [The translation of *das unmittelbare Gefühl* as "the immediate sense of religiously and ethically involved selfhood" results from a fusion of ideas gratefully borrowed from Richard R. Niebuhr, *Schleiermacher on Christ and Religion* (New York, 1964).]

CHAPTER 6

1. At this point there comes into play the faith judgment that General Superintendent Kaftan of Kiel has expressed concerning the viewpoint represented in this book. He proceeds in much the same way as the Pope did in the encyclical *Pascendi* against the Modernists, though he is far more conscientious in reproducing my modernistic teaching and in the incomparably respectable tone of his verdict. In substance, however, the two approaches are identical. The incompatibility between my doctrine and the Biblical (i.e., Pauline)-ecclesiastical position is exhibited at every point. From my disengagement of the Christian idea from its old, supernatural form it follows that I am by no means a theologian and scarcely a Christian, but am rather a Christian philosopher of religion or perhaps a Neoplatonist with a Christian tinge. No attempt is made to examine the reasons that have compelled me to accept this disengagement, to go into the natural sciences, history, or philosophy. To substantiate the separation it suffices to say: "His antisupernaturalism condemns him." In accordance with a popular theological method the reasons I advance are declared to be self-deceptive; only a nature "defined by the world," i.e., an unspiritual nature, can have induced me to draw up such reasons. The real reason is my worldly nature. But theology can hope for nothing better till it completely abandons the illusion that its methods and presuppositions have anything in common with the secular disciplines. It is certainly true that the difference between us lies at this point, and in Kaftan's sense of the term this book is not theological. In this book the question is one of truth, not of theology, and truth is taken to be accessible only on the basis of universally applicable scholarly methods. Kaftan accuses me, therefore, only of what I myself have constantly declared, and he pronounces me condemned by my "disengagement" *eo ipso*. If he does not go on to the conclusion that this division is not harmful but worthwhile, this is actually not too surprising. What the whole world of modern scholarship regards as a handicap to the Christian position I take much more seriously than a prelate of the church does, and I contend that matters are not settled by the charge of a deviation

from church doctrine or by a few Kantian turns of speech wrenched completely out of context. I am pleased, therefore, with the designation of "Christian Neoplatonist" which Kaftan has bestowed on me, the more so as one can invert it to Neoplatonic Christian. This puts me in the goodly company of the most highly educated church fathers, who of course had to face a similar charge. Also, I comfort myself with the thought that God is not the General Superintendent of the universe and therefore continue unperturbedly to regard myself as a Christian. The sense in which I understand this is shown in the present book and especially in this last section.

2. There is another direction in comparative and contrastive correlation which leads to psychology of religion and religious epistemology and thence to psychology and epistemology generally, but that approach is not at issue here. As regards this problem I refer the reader to my "Selbständigkeit der Religion" [Independence of Religion]. Of course I would be glad to give the arguments presented there a new form that would take into account the objections of my critics. Also excluded from consideration is the third major alternative, namely, working out the relationships between religious concepts and the picture of things sketched for us by modern cosmology, biology, psychology, and ethics. For the main points I must refer to my *Wissenschaftliche Lage und ihre Anforderungen an die Theologie* [The Intellectual Situation and What It Requires of Theology] (Freiburg, 1900), 49–56. I wish to add, in this connection, that this book dealt in inadequate, programmatic expressions which could become significant only with further explication. However, there are already, as a matter of fact, enough explanations of this kind. The whole of modern philosophy, insofar as it stands in a positive relation to religion, is nothing but an attempt to carry out such a program. Cf. the already mentioned works of Eucken and see also Émile Boutroux, *Science et religion dans la philosophie contemporaine* (Paris, 1908); German trans. by Emilie Weber entitled *Wissenschaft und Religion in der Philosophie unserer Zeit* [Band 10 in the series *Wissenschaft und Hypothese*] (Leipzig, 1910).

3. An interesting example of this is presented by Arthur Bonus in his essays published under the title *Zur religiösen Krisis* [The Religious Crisis], Band 1: *Zur Germanisierung des Christentums* [The Germanization of Christianity] (Jena, 1911) and Band 4: *Vom neuen Mythos* [The New Myth] (Jena, 1911). His theme is closely connected with mine, and his statements contain much that is relevant to the changes taking place in religious perception. I cannot concur, however, in his pragmatic "anti-intellectualism" or in his deriving of all religious ideas from the will to live, which means from the human subject, and the resultant evaporation of the idea of God.

4. Cf. my essay "Religion und Kirche" [Religion and Church], *Preussische Jahrbücher*, Band 81 (1895), 215–249 [reprinted in Troeltsch, *Gesammelte Schriften*, Band 2 (Tübingen, 1913), 146–182].

5. Cf. above, page 80. It is this point in particular which is decisive as over against the claim-theology (*Anspruchstheologie*) of the Ritschlian school, which I myself originally shared and from which I have eliminated the alleged analogies and parallels.

6. With regard to the Christian character affirmed of this perspective, cf. also my essay on "Die Zukunftsmöglichkeiten des Christentums" [Christianity's Future Possibilities], *Logos*, Band 1 (1910–1911), 165–185 (later reprinted in Troeltsch, *Gesammelte Schriften*, Band 2 [Tübingen, 1913], 837–862).

7. Cf., in this regard, my article "Glaube und Geschichte" [Faith and History] in *Religion in Geschichte und Gegenwart* and also my lecture *Die Bedeutung der Geschichtlichkeit Jesu für den Glauben* [The Significance of the Historicity of Jesus for Faith] (Tübingen, 1911). See also Karl Beth's criticism of these two writings in "Die Bindung des Glaubens an die Person Jesu" [The

Binding of Faith to the Person of Jesus], *Theologische Rundschau*, 15. Jahrgang (1912), 1–21. Beth believes that there is a contradiction between these
two works and calls the viewpoint of the second external and arbitrary. So it
may seem to a dogmatician who seeks to deduce logically necessary results
from presupposed universal concepts. My starting point, however, is a purely
practical and historical perspective in which what is psychologically necessary
often serves as the point of departure for the conceptually necessary. The
eternal and abstract connections I leave to the dogmaticians, who know more
about these matters than I do. It is only natural that such a perspective should
entail important consequences for the idea and practice of religious community. This I have shown in my *Die Trennung von Staat und Kirche* [The
Separation of Church and State] (Tübingen, 1905) and in my *Soziallehren der
christlichen Kirchen und Gruppen* (Tübingen, 1912) [translated by Olive Wyon
as *The Social Teaching of the Christian Churches* (London and New York,
1931)].

ERNST TROELTSCH (1865–1923), theologian and philosopher, was the leading representative of the History of Religions movement. His life theme was the problem of historicism. It permeated nearly all of his writings but was dealt with most comprehensively in two books, *Der Historismus und seine Probleme* (Historical Relativism and Its Problems) and *The Absoluteness of Christianity and the History of Religions*.

The latter, written early in Troeltsch's career, was considered by Troeltsch to be the starting point of his thought, the embryo of all that followed. As a pioneer work in the field of thinking theologically about the relationship between Christianity and other religions, *The Absoluteness of Christianity* ranks as a minor classic of German theology.

JAMES LUTHER ADAMS, foremost Troeltsch scholar in the United States, in his introduction places the book in the context of Troeltsch's total thought and the present religious scene.

DAVID REID, the translator, is Professor of the Study of Religion at Japan Biblical Seminary, Tokyo.